Level The Playing Field

The Help You've Been Searching For...

MW01610384

Resources For Getting Through Life Situations

Tiffany R. Love

Petra Consulting and Publishing
Publishing •Writing •Researching •Translating
www.trypetra.com

Library of Congress Cataloging in Publication Data

Love, Tiffany
Leveling The Playing Field : The Help You've Been Searching For /
Tiffany R. Love

p. cm.

Includes index.
ISBN 0-97122429-0-9
1. Self Improvement - Self Help - Social Services

First Edition
Printed in the United States of America

Petra Consulting and Publishing
23441 Golden Springs Drive #280
Diamond Bar, CA 91765
www.trypetra.com

To purchase this book on the World Wide Web log onto:
www.LevelingThePlayingField.com

Leveling The Playing Field

The Help You've Been Searching For...

Resources For Getting Through Life Situations

This book is dedicated to the lives of three wonderful persons whose determination, wisdom and courage transcended their earthly shells: Dr. Merri Morgan-Smith, David Eckhart, and, my most beloved uncle, Reginald Love.

I deeply miss you...

A special thank you to Mrs. Shirley C. for entering all the data contained in this book.

Other Leveling The Playing Field Books:

Leveling The Playing Field: Resources For Parents, Children, and Teens ($24.95 US)

Leveling The Playing Field: Resources For Women ($24.95 US)

Leveling The Playing Field: Resources For Seniors ($24.95 US)

Leveling The Playing Field: Resources For Marriage, Divorce, and Children of Divorced Parents ($12.95 US)

Leveling The Playing Field: Legal Resources ($24.95 US)

Leveling The Playing Field: Financial Planning, Home Buying, Selling and Refinancing ($29.95 US)

Order Online at:
www.LevelingThePlayingField.com
Or fax your order by completing the order form at the end of this book.

Attention Schools

Petra Publishing and Consulting books are available at quantity discounts with bulk purchase for educational, business, or sales promotions use. For information, please contact Petra Publishing and Consulting at the address above.

Table of Contents

CHAPTER 5 137

Employment, Unemployment and Self-Employment

CHAPTER 6 169

Doctors, Dentists, and

Ophthalmologist 169

CHAPTER 7 189

Renting, Leasing, Purchasing and Refinancing Property

CHAPTER 8

Consumer Advocacy

CHAPTER 9

Financial Problems and Repair

CHAPTER 10

Married, Unmarried, Separated, and Divorced

CHAPTER 11

Attorneys, Paralegals, and Self-Representation

CHAPTER 12

Victims, Criminals, and Accused

CHAPTER 13

Financial Planning and Understanding Financial Terms

About This Book

When action grows unprofitable, gather
[good] information; when information grows
unprofitable, sleep.
Ursula K. LeGuin

Searching for information can be painstaking, frustrating and disappointing. Thousands of resources are available, but wondering where to begin oftentimes defeats searchers before they start. *Leveling The Playing Field* has removed the hurdles by providing multiple resources for each topic.

Having access to multiple resources such as people, books, web sites, and agencies, to assist with identifying and verifying information, leads one to finding the exact help one needs. *Leveling The Playing Field* encompasses information found from three sources (books, web sites, and agencies) for just about any situation. Think of needing to find information that can help you with any given problem, instead of spending hours in the library, hours on the web or searching through bookstore shelves you can reach for one book: *Leveling The Playing Field: The Help You've Been Searching* to get answers.

Clear, concise and easy to use, *Leveling The Playing Field* is a helpful companion to inquisitive minds at every stage of life. Created especially to serve the needs of a wide variety of readers irrespective of age, ethnicity, disability, sexuality or religion.

The web site www.LevelingThePlayingField.com is an excellent companion to this book. The web site contains links, latest news feed as well as feedback information.

HOW THE CHAPTERS ARE ARRANGED

Leveling The Playing Field is arranged according to life experiences · beginning with the creation of life and ending with death. The chapters follow the common progression of experiences that we all have or will face. For each of the 400 + topics there are, at least, three resources using books, web sites, and/or agencies to ensure that you locate the desired information.

A description of the topic contained within each is section is included along with notes and a section on how the information was found to help readers expand their search beyond this book.

THE DISCLAIMER

Although the author and publisher have exhaustively researched all sources to ensure the accuracy and completeness of the information contained in this book, we assume no responsibility for errors, inaccuracies, omissions, or any inconsistency herein. Any slights of people or organizations are unintentional. Readers should use their own judgment or consult an expert in the given profession for specific remedies.

At the time of printing all links contained in this guide are active and all agency names and addresses were verified. Agencies and companies change locations and telephone numbers frequently. When contacting a company, please verify that the information is accurate.

We would like to know if you were unable to locate a resource or if you would like for us to consider a resource for our next edition. Please contact us at:

Petra Consulting and Publishing
23441 Golden Springs Drive #280
Diamond Bar, CA 91765
E-mail: contact@LevelingThePlayingField.com
Web: www.LevelingThePlayingField.com

About the Resources Contained in This Book

The book, web site, and agency references contained in this book are not paid advertisements. Neither the author nor publisher received payments, monetary or otherwise, from agencies or authors for inclusion in this book. The author performed common research techniques that any person would use to obtain all resources. The method is fully disclosed for each chapter. Neither the author nor the publisher bears any responsibility for the agency actions or lack of. For expert referrals consult a professional in the pertinent field.

Thousands of nationwide resources are available for every for any given subject matter. Consult with your local and state elected officials for locating alternative resources within your community.

The Agencies Listed

Many of the agencies listed throughout this book offer referral assistance to programs throughout the country. In most cases, the addresses to the agencies are provided in the event persons want to correspond via postal mail or e-mail rather than call. Please contact them for information regarding their services.

LOCATING OUT OF PRINT BOOKS

Spending hours searching for the right book can lead to the discovery that it's no longer available. Do not despair; there are multiple methods to locate out of print books.

- Most major bookstores have connections to independent bookstores around the country that specialize in selling out of print books and rare titles. Ask the bookstore representative for assistance locating an out of print book. Major chains may have unsold copies located at other branch stores, which can be shipped to your local bookstore at no additional cost. Call more than one bookstore; some are more knowledgeable and helpful than others. Specialty bookstores are particularity helpful at locating hard to find books.

- Another method is to contact the publisher directly to order a copy of the book. Oftentimes the publisher will have extra copies in stock. If enough demand exists, the book could be reprinted. Ask the bookstore clerks for the name, address, telephone number, web site, and email address of the publisher. Get as much contact information as possible. If you are unable to obtain contact information, you can search online for the publisher through R. R. Bowker, which has an entire listing of publishers. Log onto www.bowker.com for more information.

Locating out of print books online

During my writing I discovered that a book I referenced is out of print, [1] *What to do when you can't afford health care* by Matthew Lesko. I wanted to include it as a reference so I ordered it online using the following link; www.elephantbooks.com, this is only one of hundreds of used and rare booksellers online.

---

[1] What to do when you can't afford health care, Matthew Lesko, ©1993, Published by Information USA Inc.

Introduction

Accurate information is a key part of motivation

Mary Ann Allison

One night I arrived home from work exhausted from staring at a computer for eight hours and later rushing through bumper-to-bumper traffic in an attempt to arrive home, eat, fall asleep, and repeat the same scenario the following day. Feeling like my daily activities were monotonous and void of purpose, I turned on the television in hopes of watching something that would refocus my thinking from myself and onto something useless in order to quickly fall asleep. The news program, 60 Minutes®, was on. I watched Ed Bradley's interview with a young man, only 13 years old, in jail awaiting trial for murdering a neighborhood child. At the time of the crime he was 11 years old. The interviewer asked the mother of the accused questions about seeking help for her son before the murder transpired. She listed all the agencies from which she sought help: the police, school, and counselors all to no avail; they admitted that she looked for help from them and no one provided her with assistance. My heart turned from sadness to anger at the thought of the thousands of resources available, and no one told her how to find them. It was this event that inspired me to write a book to ensure that any man, woman or child receives information when they need it the most.

Searching for help is difficult because it is hard to determine where to begin with so much information available in this information world. This book takes a huge pile of data and sorts it according to life experiences. It would be difficult, to include every resource into one book; however, I strived to eliminate the confusion of where to start by including hundreds of resources, notes, and a section on how the information was found. With some initiative locating the right help is made easier.

Before you begin, there are a few tools you will need:

- Access to a computer (see "Using the Internet to Locate Resources" in this chapter. You do not have to own a computer to use the Internet).
- An ink pen, pencil, and paper.
- A pleasant attitude (getting help only hurts when you are upset. At the same time, there are times to get upset-- remember to pick and choose your battles carefully).
- Perseverance - DO NOT QUIT! This is the most important tool you'll need.
- A form of communicating (mouth, sign language, letter, etc).

That's all!

LOCATING RESOURCES

Locating information is similar to walking through a maze; there is a beginning and an end. Every wrong turn teaches something; it may only be where not to look. By applying instinct, knowledge, and luck, you'll reach the end. It can be lots of fun as many people make a career out of locating hard to find information. You don't need to be a pro, just be persistent. Learn from every call – be patient some people simply don't know how to help you. That's why it's important to communicate your objective clearly to others: keep it simple. If there is a dire need tell the representative in less than 30 seconds, that may motivate them to go the extra mile or they may find the one person who can assist you right away.

Using the Internet to Locate Resources

The Internet has a wealth of resources and information. If you do not have a computer, most libraries (public, college, and law libraries) will allow you to use public computers at no charge. You may need an appointment to use these systems. Contact your local library for information about computer privileges for the public. Don't forget your job. Companies typically allow workers to use the Internet for general surfing and researching as long as it doesn't lead to loss hours of work time and surfing pornography sites. If you work in an area that doesn't have a computer with Internet access, ask your boss if he/she can arrange computer time for use during non-working hours such as lunch and break times.

Community based computer centers allow person to utilize computers for a specified period of time. You may need to make an appointment and there may be a small fee to use the computer. Other centers around the county provide access to public

Locating Internet Cafes www.netcafes.com

computers for free or a nominal fee, which may be waived depending on your economic condition. A current trend is coffee houses with computers available for public use. Also, a friend or relative could be of assistance. Many Americans have at least one computer in their homes.

Once you have gained access to a computer, open an e-mail account, if the Internet Service Provider (ISP) has not already been provided one. Many sites provide free email and dial-up access. Try the following site for email service: mail.yahoo.com, www.juno.com, www.gte-mail.net. Try the following for free dial-up access: www.worldshare.com, www.netzero.com, www.zdnet.com. Fee dial up services may take longer than normal to connect, but remember you can't beat the price.

Location	Sources
Books	Lake, Matthew. *I'm on the Internet Now What?!* Marboro Books, p. 208 Paperback. © 2001. Cadenhead, Rogers. *How To Use the Internet:* 2002 Edition © 2001. Cooper, Brian and Annalisa Milner and Tim Worsley. *Essential Internet Guide.* D K Publishing, p. 280 Hardcover, © 2001.
Web sites	www.ispcheck.com www.learnthenet.com www.internet101.org www.netlingo.com

OTHER METHODS FOR LOCATING RESOURCES

When looking for help it, is advisable to begin by asking people you know questions on how to locate resources for your specific need. My hairdresser, for instance, interacts with people in many different professions throughout the day. She has proven to be an excellent resource to me. Family members and friends are another excellent resource, because of their professions they are exposed to others in the community who can direct me to the information I need.

Clergy, lawyers, law enforcement officers, doctors, nurses, school counselors, and teachers, as well as other professionals are also knowledgeable sources. Moreover, I highly encourage everyone to contact local and state elected officials. As your representative, they become informed of the types of help their constituents need in addition they can see to it that the desired help is located or created to serve their community.

Locating information in books

The library has many resource books available for reviewing and/or loaning, typically older outdated resource books are loaned. From experience I've found that current reference books are not allowed for lending only viewing. Librarians are helpful aids to researching material. Just tell them the subject matter and they will be able to assist you with locating information. It is best to call the library in advance if the information requires long hours of research time. For best results, call or visit the library during children school hours for the least amount of interruptions. When there are many people waiting it is difficult to give everyone the same amount of attention. Once you have found a helpful librarian, continue to use his or her services, establish a positive relationship with him/her, as you may be surprised by how much information they can obtain. Don't be limited to public libraries, law librarians are most helpful and the staff is knowledgeable. They do not give legal advice, but they know which material best addresses your situation. College libraries are also another valuable resource available to the public.

As of the last five years, bookstores have become as efficient as libraries at locating information. In the past the staff was often preoccupied with various customers; they typically performed a search on the computer and rapidly muttered the isle section where the title was last spotted. Although this is still the practice of a few bookstores more are providing personalized service; they walk you to the location where the book can be found and direct you to other books along the same topic. As previously mentioned, some bookstores can help with finding out of print and rare titles. Similar to libraries there are better times to go to the bookstore for performing extensive research. Early morning and mid afternoon, after shifts have changed, are the best times.

Chapter 1

Pregnancy

*Moving between the legs of tables and of
chairs, Rising or falling, grasping at kisses
and toys, Advancing boldly, sudden to take
alarm, Retreating to the corner of arm and
knee, Eager to be reassured, taking pleasure
In the fragrant brilliance of the Christmas
tree . . ..*

T.S. Elliot

Expecting a baby is the most exciting yet anxious time in a woman's life. Finding support through the ups and downs for mothers-to-be is often near. A spouse, partner, parent(s), and friend(s) are all resources that prove indispensable to expectant parents.

☼How The Information Was Found

The information found in this chapter was obtained by research from a combination of sources. The primary source was the Internet, libraries, and bookstores. Using the Internet, I preformed a search for each of the topics provided. For example, for pregnancy planning I typed *Pregnancy Plan*. Many results appeared, so I eliminated the resources I thought were least helpful.

Using the library and bookstores, I located several resource books for pregnancy. Much of the material is useful, providing illustrations and additional resources. To my delight I discovered books that are dedicated to finding resources for pregnant women, those titles are provided throughout this chapter.

I found a wealth of the birthing and pregnancy support organizations by reading the newspapers. Local newspapers carry news releases, of community organizations hosting award programs, meeting, symposiums, etc. For example, a local organization, Sister Friend (not mentioned in this nationwide guide), was obtained after I read an article in a free paper. I was impressed with their objective, so I scheduled time to attend one of their symposiums. The others were located by utilizing library resources.

I must say that pregnancy by far is the most well documented experience one can have. If you want to know anything about pregnancy, the information is abundantly available for both men and women.

PLANNING FOR A PREGNANCY

Throughout many women and men's lives they one-day dream of having a child. Once the time comes for planning a pregnancy, the expectation can seem overwhelming. If you are considering becoming pregnant, careful planning is the bridge to assist you with the emotional and physical aspects of parenthood.

What to expect

Be of good cheer, there is an abundance of information on *what to expect* during your pregnancy. Including hundreds of books and websites that have detailed information such as pictures of every stage of the baby's development. Many web sites contain ovulation calculators and pregnancy calendars for predicting the baby's arrival. Another valuable resource is your practitioner; he/she can answer your questions, recommend books, provide you with pamphlets as well as refer you to agencies offering support groups for additional help. The resources within this chapter represent a small fraction of the vast amount of valuable resources available.

Location	Source	
Books	Landi, Nina D. *125 Things You Must Know About Being Pregnant.* Paperback. Owl Books, © 1998.	Iovine, Vicki. *The Girl Friend's Guide to Pregnancy: Or Everything Your Doctor Won't Tell You.* Paperback, © 1995.
	Sussman, John R. MD. , Levitt B. Blake. *Before You Conceive: The Complete Pregnancy Guide.* Bantam	Sears, William and Martha Sears, *The Baby Book: Everything You Need To Know About Your Baby From Birth to Age Two.*

Location	Source	
	Doubleday Dell, Paperback. © 1989.	Little Brown and Company, © 1993.
	Eisenberg, Arlene, Heidi E. Murkoff and Sandee Hathaway Eisenberg. *The What to Expect When You're Expecting Pregnancy Organizer Spiral Edition* Workman Publishing Company. © 1995.	Louden, Jennifer. *The Pregnant Woman's Comfort Book. Harper San Francisco* ©1995. *During Pregnancy and Early Motherhood p.240.* Harper San Francisco, © 1995.
Web	www.babiesonline.com www.4babies.com www.babyzone.com www.familyweb.com www.childbirth.org	www.momsonline.com www.obgyn.net www.babiestoday.com www.thelaboroflove.com www.makewayforbaby.com
Agencies	**National Institute of Child Health and Human Development (NIH)** Building 31, Room 2132 9000 Rockville Pike Bethesda, MD 20892 (301) 496-5133	**Maternity Center Association** 48 E. 92nd Street New York, NY 10128 **Family Service American** 11700 W. Lake Park Dr. Milwaukee, WI 53224

Prenatal Care

Prenatal care is a culmination of many services provided primarily to the mother while pregnant. These services include regular visits to a practitioner, nutrition information, and exercise plans including, information regarding maternity assistance. Receiving prenatal care is essential to your child having a healthy beginning in life. Once you become aware that you are pregnant it is recommended that you begin receiving early and regular health care treatment by trained professionals.

Location	Sources
Books	Stoppard, Miriam. *Prenatal Care.* Dorling Kindersley Publishing Inc. Paperback p.80. © 1998. De Crespigny, Lachlan & Rhonda Dredge. *Which Test For My Unborn Baby? Ultrasound and other Prenatal Tests.* Oxford University Press. p.188. © 1996. Stanley, Thomas H. *Expecting Trouble: The Myth of Prenatal Care in America.* New York University Press, Hardcover p.300. © 2000.
Web	www.babyzone.com www.childbirth.com www.blackwomenhealth.com www.obgyn.net www.w-cpc.org/pregnancy www.pregnancytoday.com www.4women.gov www.plannedparenthood.org
Agencies	**Health Mothers, Healthy Babies (HMHB)** (202) 863-2458 409 21st Street SW., Suite 309 Washington, DC 20024 **National Women's Information Center** (800) 94409662 (888) 220-5446(TDD) 850 Arlington Blvd. Suite 300 Fairfax, VA 22031 **March of Dimes Birth Defects Foundation** 1275 Mamaroneck Ave. White Plains, NY 10605 (914) 428-7100 **International Childbirth Education Association** P. O. Box 20048 Minneapolis, MN 55420 **Planned Parenthood Federation of America** 810 Seventh Ave.

Location	Sources
	New York, NY 10019
	(212) 541-7800
	(800) 230-PLAN

BABY PRODUCTS

It is never too soon to begin purchasing baby products, even one year before a baby arrives. Thousands of baby products are in the market, choosing the safest product for your newborn has become a daunting task. The following resources can help with identifying safe products for your bundle of joy.

Location	Source	
Books	Pennybacker, Mindy. *Mothers & Others For a Livable Planet Guide to Natural Baby Care: Nontoxic and Environmentally Friendly Ways to Take Care of Your New Child.* © 1999. Krantz, Les, Sharon Ludman- Exley. *The Best of Everything For your Baby: Rating and Reviews on Everything From Diapers and Car Seats to Baby Monitors and Cribs.* Prentice Hall Press. © 1999. Consumer Reports Books 7ᵗʰ Edition. *Guide To Baby Products.* 2001.	Fields, Denise & Alan Fields. *Baby Bargains 4Ed.* Windsor Peak Press. © 2001. Los Angeles Baby Resource Guide. *I'm Expecting.* First Edition, Hazen Publishing © 1998. Wise, Debra. *Baby Gear: Everything You Need to Know to Clothe, Feed, Transport, Protect, Entertain, and Care for Your Baby to Age Three.* Griffen Trade Paper Back, © 2001. Jones, Sandy. *Guide to Baby Products.* Paperback, © 2001.

Location	Source	
Web	www.thebabyguide.com www.superbabyfood.com www.cpsc.gov www.happybaby www.greatbabyproducts.com www.baby-products.com www.babyestore.com	
Agencies	**National Women's Health Information Center** 850 Arlington Blvd. Suite 300 Fairfax, VA 22031 (800) 994-9662 (888) 226-5446 (TTD) **Consumer Product Safety Commission (CPSC)** Washington, DC 20207 (800) 638-CPSC (800) 638-(TDD)	**Juvenile Products Manufacturers Association (JPMA)** Two Green Tree Center, Suite 225 Marlton, NJ 08053 (609) 985-2878

Parenting Classes

See Parenting Classes in Chapter 2

Recall of Products

With many recalls of baby products you may need help locating the safest product for you new baby. The following resources are valuable for locating safe baby products.

Location	Source
Books	Felcher, Marla E. *It's No Accident: How Corporations Sell Dangerous Baby Products.* Common Courage Press. Paperback p.302. © 2001. Jones, Sandy. *Guide to Baby Products.* Paperback. © 2001. Brandenburg, Mark A. MD. *Child Safe: A Practical Guide To Preventing Childhood Injuries.* Three River Press © 2000.
Web	www.notice.com www.babybag.com www.csps.gov www.fda.gov www.Consumerreports. org www.defectivebabyproducts.com www.greatbabyproducts.com www.happybaby.com www.thenewparents.com www. Pueblo.ssa.gov
Agencies	**American Academy of Pediatrics** 141 Northwest Point Blvd. Box 927 Elk Grove Village, IL 60009 (312) 228-5005 **Federal Consumer Information Center (FCIC)** Pueblo, CO 81009 (800) 688-9889 TTY (800) 326-2996 **Consumer Reports Guide to Baby products** (800) 638-2772	**U.S. Consumer Product Safety Commission** 4330 East-West Highway Bethesda, Maryland 20814-4408 (301) 504-0990 **Consumer Union of US** 101 Truman Ave Yonkers, NY 10703-1057 (914) 378-2000

Location	Source
	The National Highway Traffic Safety Administration (Child Car seats) 400 7th St. SW Washington, DC 20590 (888) DASH-2-Dot (Toll Free Hot Line)

HOUSING, FOOD, AND CLOTHING

Should you require assistance with obtaining housing, clothing baby furniture, pampers, car seat(s), and other necessities, agencies exists for the primary purpose of assisting mothers in need.

Location	Source	
Web	www.all-free-samples.com www.4women.gov www.freestuffonline.com www.bethany.org www.covenanthouse.org www.pregnancycenters.org www.catholiccharitiesusa.org www.bestfreestuffonline.com	
Agencies	**Pregnancy Help line** **Liberty Godparent Home** P.O. Box 4199 Lynchburg, VA 24502 (800) 542-4453 **Pregnancy Hotline National** 686 N. Broad Street Woodbury, NJ 08096	**Bethany Christian Services National** P.O. Box 294 Grand Rapids, MI 49501 (800) BETHANY (800) 238-4269 (Pregnancy Crises Line) **Project Cuddle Inc.** **2973 Harbor Blvd.** Cost Mesa, CA 92626

Location	Source	
	(800) 848-5683	(888) 628-3353
		(800) 238-4269
	Liberty God Parents	
	P.O. Box 4199	**Community Action**
	Lynchburg, VA 24502	**Partnership**
	(800) 542-4453	1100 17th St. NW
	(Pregnant Teens)	Suite 500
		Washington, DC 20036
	Catholic Charities USA	(202) 265-7546
	1731 King Street, Suite 200	
	Alexandria, VA 22314	**Child Welfare League of**
	(703) 549-1390	**America**
	National Youth Crises	440 First Street, NW
	Hot Line	Washington, CA 20001
	(800) 448-4663	(202) 942-0270

PRENATAL CARE FOR LOW-INCOME FAMILIES

Many medical agencies offer free or low cost medical care to low-income families. A vast number of practitioners treat disadvantaged women, although they may limit the number of low-income patients they accept per year. Call respected practitioners in your area for information on income restrictions. Most practitioners encourage

Ask nurses, friends, and family about locating a knowledgeable practitioner. The best referrals are those who have utilized a practitioner's service. Oftentimes practitioners are pleased that current patients referred them to others.

patients to have some form of medical coverage, even if it is government sponsored. Persons experiencing difficulty locating a practitioner can contact state and federal advocacy groups that have adopted healthy family programs offering referrals to doctors who accept low-income patients.

Location	Source
Books	Los Angeles Baby Resource Guide. *I'm Expecting.* Hazen Publishing dba. First Edition © 1998.
Web	www.healthystart.net www.ehealthinsurance.com http://kidshealth.org

OBTAINING MEDICAL INSURANCE

See Obtaining Medical Insurance in Chapter 6 for more information.

LOCATING A PROFESSIONAL PRACTITIONER

Selecting a practitioner is an important part of making your pregnancy safe and comfortable. Two categories of practitioners who specialize in birthing: Physician and Nurse/Midwife. You may also decide to have a Doula present during the birthing process to provide comfort during and after labor.

Once you have selected a practitioner, interview the person before committing both you and your baby's life into their hands. To ensure that you are comfortable and secure with their experience and training, ask the practitioner questions. The practitioner should be patient with your questions and understanding of any concerns. Feel comfortable with their answers to prevent further stress during your pregnancy. Resources for this section are provided at the end of the following sub topics.

Physicians

Several types of physicians provide neonatal and prenatal care: Obstetricians Perinatologists and Family Physicians.

Family Physician

Family Physicians treat common medical occurrences that require little or no invasive treatment. Their professional training includes delivering babies, but most chose to refer this service to doctors who specialize in childbirth. Persons residing in small towns are left with no other option than their family doctor for the delivery of their babies. If complications and/or multiple births are anticipated, which are considered high-risk pregnancies; family doctors almost always refer these deliveries to specialists, regardless of their geographic location.

Obstetrician

Obstetrician or Obstetrician/Gynecologist are doctors who specialize in treating the reproductive aspects of women, pregnant women and babies up to one year old (typically, after age one the child begins treatment by a Pediatrician). Obstetricians are commonly used during delivery because they have undergone years of medical training and are experienced with the birthing process.

Perinatologists

Perinatologists specialize in obstetrics and gynecology. This arm of physicians is also referred to as Maternal Fetal Medicine; they treat high-risk pregnancies, onset pregnancy conditions, miscarriages, and abnormalities.

Location	Source
	A. Miller and R. Challender. *Obstetrics Illustrated* 5th *Edition*. Harcourt and Brace, © 1997.
Books	Beischer and Mackay. *Obstetrics and the New Born* 3rd *Edition*. Harcourt and Brace, © 1997.

Location	Source	
Web	www.ama-assn.org www.dr4lads.com www.desmonesperinatal.com www.checkbook.org www.acog.org www.familydoctor.org	
Agencies	**Center for The Study Of Services** 733 15th Street, NW Washington, DC 20005 (202) 347-7283 **American Medical Association** 515 North State Street Chicago, IL 60610 (800) 621-8335 **American Academy of Family Physicians** 11400 Tomahawk Creek Parkway Leawood, KS 66201 (800) 274-2237	**American Academy of Pediatrics** 141 Northwest Point Blvd. P.O. Box 927 Elk Grove Village, IL 60009-0927 **American College of Obstetricians and Gynecologists** 409 12th Street, SW P.O. Box 96920 Washington, DC 20090 (202) 863-2518 **American Academy of Pediatrics** 141 Northwest Point Blvd. Elk Grove Village, IL 60009-0927

Nurse/Midwife

For many years midwives have been used for delivering babies; this is a historic and honorable profession. Prior to hospitals, babies were delivered in homes with the assistance of a loved one or midwife. Currently, most midwives have registered nursing backgrounds and have specialized in obstetrics, gynecology, and newborn care. He/she may be certified as a midwife by a registration board or agency. Ask the referring agency (or midwife) of any certifications and education received.

Location	Source	
Books	Davis, Elizabeth, Suzanne Arms. *Heart and Hands: A Midwife's Guide to Pregnancy and Birth.* Celestial Arts, © 1997.	
Web	www.cfmidefery.org www.mana.org www.narm.org www.midwivesmodelofcare.org www.goodnewnet.org	
Agencies	**Midwives Alliance of North America** 4805 Lawrence Hwy. Suite 116-279 Lilburn, GA 30047 (888) 923-MANA (6262) **The American College of Nurse-Midwives** 5257 Rosestone Drive Lilburn, GA 30047 (888) 842-4784	**North American Registry of Midwives** 5252 Rosestone Dr. Lilburn, GA 30047 (888) 842-4784 **Citizens For Midwifery** P.O. Box 82227 Athens, GA 30608-2227 (888) CFM-4880

Doulas

Doulas are professionally trained companions who provide non- medical and non-pharmacological support, during and after the birth, to the mother. Studies that suggest that obtaining support for mothers-to-be can reduce the length of labor, prenatal problems and caesarean rates. As with all types of practitioners, carefully review the Doulas background and check references. A reputable agency can supply names and numbers of families who have utilized the Doula's assistance.

Location	Source	
Books	Simkin, Penny. *The Birth Partner.* Harvard Common Press © 2001. Bond, Antoinette, Graham, Janet M. *Doula: We Couldn't have Done It Without You*! Lambs Publishing. © 2001. Klaus, Marshall H., et al. *Mothering the Mother: How a Doula can Help You have a Shorter easier, and Healthier Birth.* Perseus Press. © 1993.	
Web	www.doula.us www.dona.com www.alace.org	
Agencies	**Doula Association** 877-4-A-Doula (423-6852) Toll-free **DONA (Doulas of North America)** 206-324-5440 1100 23rd Avenue East Seattle, WA 98112	**National Association of Childbirth Assistants** P.O. Box 1537 Boyes Hot Springs, LA 95416 707-939-0543 **Association of Labor**

Location	Source	
	email: *askdona@aol.com*	**Assistants and Child Birth Education (ALACE)** 617-441-2500 P.O. Box 382724 Cambridge, MA 02238

BREAST-FEEDING

When it comes to feeding your newborn there is <u>no</u> equivalent substitute for mother's milk. Feeding your baby naturally has proven to provide immunities to diseases and reduce instances of SIDS (Sudden Infant Death Syndrome) as well as preventing viruses, infections and diseases that could occur later in life. It should be a mother's first choice to provide the best possible nutrients to her baby and breastfeeding is second to none. Not only is it beneficial to the baby, but to the mother as well. Breastfeeding helps the uterus to contract, helps to prevent massive blood loss, and helps to reduce the mother's weight, moreover, it's free. Some reports that suggest that breastfeeding can help prevent uterine and breast cancers.

Location	Source	
Books	Renfrew, Fisher and Arms; *Breastfeeding: Getting Breastfeeding Right For You*: Illustrated Guide. Celestial Arts, © 1990. Wilson-Clay, Barbara, Kay Hoover. *The Breastfeeding Atlas.* Leaven © 2000.	Sears, Martha, RN and William Sears, MD. *The Breastfeeding Book.* Leaven © 2001. Lang, Sandra. *Breastfeeding Special Care Babies.* Leaven © 2000.

Location	Source	
	Kerkhoff, Karen. *Mothering Multiples: Breastfeeding and Caring for Twins or More!!!* Revised Edition, La Leche League. © 1999.	Gotsch, Gwen, Judy Torgus. *The Womanly Art of Breastfeeding.* Plume. ©1997. Newman, Jack, Teresa Pitman *The Ultimate Breastfeeding Book of Answers* . Prima Publishing © 2000.
Web	www.breastfeeding.com www.lalecheleague.org	www.promom.org www.icla.org
Agencies	**The La Leche League International** 1400 N. Meacham Road P.O. Box 4079 Schaumburg, IL. 60168-4079 (800) 525-3243 **International Lactation Consultant Association (ILCA)** 1500 Sunday Drive, Suite 102 Raleigh, NC 27607 (919) 787-5181	**Promotion for Mother's Milk (Pro MoM), Inc.** P.O. Box 3912 New York, NY 10163 **National Women Health Information Center** Suite 300 Fairfax, VA 22031 (800) 994-9662 (888) 220-5446 (Hearing Impaired)

Breastfeeding at work

Several alternatives to feeding your baby from the breast are available, particularly when you are away at work. Many mothers express their milk prior to work and during lunch breaks. Different types of equipment that range in price are available to assist with expressing milk. Some companies rent breast pumps and other nursing equipment for a fee. Verify with your insurance plan for information on payment or reimburse for the costs for breastfeeding products and pumps. If you are a [2]WIC recipient you may qualify to receive free products.

EXPECTING FATHERS

Dad is one of the important members of the pregnancy team. He provides comfort and support while the mother-to-be body undergoes unfamiliar transformations. Similar to expecting mothers, impending fatherhood can cause different emotions for men. To prepare for the expectations and demands of pregnancy it is important to schedule time to accompany your partner on visits to the practitioner and assist with prenatal care activities such as Lamaze. Do not hesitate to ask questions, be curious, and participant in the pregnancy.

Location	Source	
Books	Goldman, Marcus Jacob MD. *The Joy of Fatherhood.* Prima Publishing. © 2000.	At Home Dad (newsletter) 61 Brightwood Avenue N. Andover, MA. 01845-1702
	Aaron, Hass Ph.D. *The Gift of Fatherhood: How Men Lives Are Transformed by Their Children*: Simon & Schuster. © 1994.	Email: athomedad@aol.com Williams, Gene B. *The New Fathers Panic Book: Everything a Dad Needs to Know to Welcome His*

---

[2] WIC (Women Infants and Children) is a program that provides educational resources for women of all ages in addition to vouchers for women to receive milk and milk by products, foods, and baby products.

Location	Source	
	Canfield, Ken R. *Seven Secrets of Effective Fathers*. Tyndal House Publishers. © 1993. Marzallo, Jean. *Fathers and Babies: How Babies Grow and What they need from you from birth to 18 months*. Harper Trade. © 1998.	*Bundle of Joy*. Aaron Books © 1997. Bruce, Linton. *Finding Time for Fatherhood: The Important Considerations Men Face When They Become Parents*. Father's Forum Press. © 1990. Brott, Armin A. & Jennifer Ash. *The Expectant Father: Facts, Tips and advice for Dads-To-Be*. Abbeville Press HC&PB. P.216 © 1995.
Web	www.fathers.com www.fatherwork.byu.edu/bith.htm. www.fathersnetwork.org www.responsiblefatherhood.org www.fatherhoodproject.org www.fatherhood.org www.acfc.org www.cyfc.umn.edu/fathernet www.bamin.org www.menstuff.org www.fathermag.com www.fathersfourm.com www.dadscan.org	
Agencies	**National Center for Fathering** **Father's Hotline (referral to organizations)** **(512) 472-DADS (3237)** email: dads@fathers.org **National Center on Fathers and Families** C/O University of	**Father's Resource Center** 430 Oak Grove Street, Suite 105 Minneapolis, MN 55403 (612) 874-1509 **National Center for Fathering** 10200 W. 75th Street

Location	Source
Pennsylvania 3700 Walnut Street, Box 58 Philadelphia, PA 19104-6216 Tel: (215) 898-5000	#267 Shawnee Mission, KS 66204-2223 Tel:(913) 384-4661 Tel: (913) 384-4665 Email: nfc@aol.com

Paternity and Maternity Leave

Paternity leave allows a spouse to take a [paternity] leave up to one year, without affecting benefits. Many people choose not to take advantage of this law because employers are not obligated to pay wages during the time off from work, however, employers are required to pay sick time and vacation balances. Employers may require notice in advance prior to taking Paternity

> The Family and Medical Leave Act also apply to persons who have adopted children.

Leave, typically three to four weeks in order to arrange for adequate staff coverage. If your leave is greater than 90 days there is no guarantee that your position will be the same; however, it must be the equivalent of that held prior to your departure, including the same compensation and benefits. Your employer cannot lawfully terminate you for exercising your right to take a paternity leave. Contact a knowledgeable attorney in the field of employment law for more information.

Location	Source
Books	Decker, Kart H. *Family and Medical Leave In A Nut Shell.* West Information Publisher Group, © 2000.

Location	Source
	Holcomb, Betty. *The Best Friend's Guide to Maternity Leave: Making The Most of Your Precious Time at Home.* Perseus Book © 2001. Weisberg, Anne A., Buckler Carol A. *Everything A Working Mother Needs to Know* Main Street Books © 1994. (This title is currently out of print – try contacting the publisher)
Web	www.workingmother.com www.workingwomanmag.com www.americanbaby.com www.womenswire.com www.fmla.com
Agencies	**The Woman's Bureau** (800) 827-5335 TDD 1- 400-326-2577. The Woman's Bureau is head quartered in Washington, DC and has regional offices throughout the US that provides referral services **Department of labor Wage and hour Referral Line** (866) 4USWAGE (866) 487-9243

Alternative Agency Resources

For more information regarding paternity and maternity leave contact your companies Human Resources Department and your state Department of Labor Office.

PREGNANT WOMEN IN THE WORK PLACE

Laws, both state and federal, are designed to protect women rights during pregnancy. Most companies are progressive and abide by laws that guard expecting mothers rights.

Nonetheless, being aware of your rights helps to avoid unnecessary stress that can adversely affect you and your baby's health. For an expansive research on rights of pregnant women contact agencies identified in this section.

Location	Source
Books	Sack, Steven Mitchell. *The Working Woman's Legal Survival Guide.* Prentice Hall Press, © *1998*
	www.eeoc.gov www.dol.gov/wb/
Agencies	**EEOC** (Equal Employment Opportunity Commission) (800) 669-EEOC **The Woman's Bureau** (800) 827-5335 TDD 1- 400-326-2577. The Woman's Bureau is head quartered in Washington, DC and has regional offices throughout the US that provides referral services **U.S. Department of Justice** **Civil Rights Division** PO Box 65998 Washington, DC 20035-5998 (202) 514-4713 Fax: (202) 514-1116

Pregnancy Discrimination

According to the Pregnancy Discrimination Act of 1978, the Civil Rights Act of 1968, and the Civil Rights Act of 1991, expecting a baby should not prohibit your from obtaining employment, being turned down for a promotion, receiving benefits and being laid off/fired. To read more about these laws and to find more information visit the EEOC web site at: www.eeoc.gov

PREGNANT MINORS

Having a baby is a wonderful blessing. Being prepared for the baby's arrival is essential to the newborns healthy start.

The excitement and preparation for childbirth is the same as with all women and men regardless of age. For young women and men choosing to have a baby is decision met with more obstacles than their older counterparts. Young women and men likewise are expected to be accountable for the material and physical needs of the baby, which can be difficult for adolescents who have not begun living independently from their parents. Within this section you'll find resources specific to teenage pregnancy: however, all of the resources contained in this chapter and throughout this book are available to all expecting families regardless of age.

Locating Resources For Minors

School counselors are available to assist adolescents through calm or crises. Counselors have access of local resources that assist teenage students in need of help. Ask your counselor for resource books to help with identifying programs specific to your needs.

In most cases pregnant minors are not to be given *special* treatment academically. For as long as the student can attend school she is expected to meet curriculum objectives. When the student is no longer able to attend class arrangements for completing course work must be made: schoolwork planning typically occurs once the student notifies the school of her pregnancy.

Location	Source
Books	Endersbe, Julie K. *Teen Fathers: Getting Involved.* Lifeline Maters Press, © 2000. Endersbe, Julie K. *Teen Mothers: Raising a Baby.* Lifeline Matters Press, © 2000. Ewing, Bergmann Ann. *Day Care and Diplomas: Teen Mothers Who Stayed In School.* Fairview Press, © 2001.
Web	www.childbrith.org www.teenpregnancy.org www.npin.org www.parentingteens.com www.pregnancycenters.org www.youngfamilies.org www.fatherhood.org www.bu.edu/cohis/teenpreg/teenpreg.htm
Agencies	**National Fatherhood Initiative** 101 Lake Forest Blvd. Suite 360 Gaithersburg, MD 20877 (301) 948-0599 **Alliance For Young Families** 105 Chauncy Street 8th Floor Boston, MA 02111 (617) 482-9122

Often physical restraints such as physical education (PE) classes exist for expecting teen mothers. Pregnant students are asked not to participate or given light activities. Exposure to chemicals that could potentially harm the baby such as those produced during chemistry classes is another factor to consider when planning for academic alternatives. Classes of this nature may require make up or enrollment in an alternative course or school.

PREGNANCY LOSS

Losing a baby is an expecting parents worse nightmare. The grief associated with a loss of an unborn baby varies. Some women do not experience any grief, while a spouse may have a difficult time coming to terms with the loss. This variance in emotion does not determine the amount of caring or love one has for the baby as it is common for people to have different perspectives on a lost during pregnancy. For persons who feel sorrow, it is important to allow yourself to grieve the loss of an unborn baby. Seek comfort from those who understand the value of your emotions. The following resources are available to assist persons with their grief.

Location	Source	
Web	www.misschildren.org www.nationalshareoffice.com www.Sids-network.org www.drdaiter.com/pregtable.htm www.stillfathers.org	
Agencies	**SIDS Alliance** 1314 Bedford Ave. Suite 210 Baltimore, MD 21208 (800) 221-7437	**American SIDS Institute** 2480 Windy Hill Road Suite 380 Marietta, GA 30067 (800) 232-7337
	AMEND (Aiding A Mother and Father Experiencing Neonatal Death) 4324 Berrywick Terrace St. Louse, MO 63128 (314) 487-7582	**SIDS Information** Clearinghouse 2070 Chain Bridge Road Suite 450 Vienna, VA 22182 (703) 821-8955
	National Share Office St. Joseph Health Center	

Location	Source
	300 First Capital Drive St. Charles, MO 63301-2893 (800) 821-6819

SUBSTANCE ABUSE

To ensure that your baby has the best chance for survival and a healthy life, parents must take precautions as to what substances they take into their bodies. Mothers who are addicted or casually using drugs, can contact the following resources for help *(many of the agencies listed below can offer referral services to programs nearest to your area)*:

Location	Source	
Web	www.aloholics-anonymous.org www.12steps.org www.quitesmokingsupport.com	www.well.com www.cmhc.com www.additions.net
Agencies	**National Drug & Alcohol Treatment Referral Routing** (800) 662-4357 **National Council on Alcohol and Drug Dependencies** (800) 622-2255 **Project Cuddle, INC** 2973 Harbor Blvd Costa Mesa, CA 92626	**888 Marijuana** (888) 627-4502 **CAST (Center for Substance Abuse Treatment) Hotline** (800) 662-4357 **Drug Help** C/O Phoenix House 164 W. 74th Street New York, NY 10023 (800) 378-4435 (800) Drug Help

Location	Source
	(888) 628-3353
	American Council on Alcoholism 3900 N. Fairfax Dr., Suite 401 Arlington, VA 22203 (800) 527-5344

INFERTILITY

Many couples are unable to have children *naturally*. Options are available to those who desire to birth a child using non-traditional methods. Options include invetro-fertilization, artificial insemination and surgery. The following resources provide detailed information about the choices.

Location	Source	
Web	www.inciid.org www.fertiltext.org www.sharedjourney.com	www.ivf.com www.fertilityplus.org www.resolve.org
Agencies	**The International Council on Infertility Information Dissemination (INCIID)** P.O. Box 6836, Arlington, Virginia 22206 Phone: (703) 379-9178 **The National Infertility Association** 1310 Broadway Somerville MA 02144 (888) 623-0744	

BABY'S DEFECTS AND DISABILITIES

Many birth defects are detected prior to the delivery of the baby. This affords parents the option to continue or discontinue the pregnancy. Being informed of a possible danger to your baby is traumatic. Having the support of family and friends is vital to determining the best course of action for you and your family. For some there is no doubt about their decision while other may be tormented by the choices. It's important to take time, if possible, to research all options before committing to a decision.

Location	Source
Books	Schiff, Donald. et.al. *American Academy of Pediatrics:* *The Official, Complete Home Reference Guide to Your Child's Symptoms.* Villard Books. © 1997. Schmitt, Barton D. *Your Child's Health: The Parent's Guide to Symptoms, Emergencies, Common Illnesses, Behavior and School Problems.* Bantam Books. © 1991. Sears, William, MD and Martha Sears, RN. *The Fussy Baby: How To Bring The Best In Your High-Need Baby.* La Leche League International © 2000.
Web	www.exceptionalchildrenwork.com www.amp-info.net
Agencies	**Birth Defects Research For Children** (800) 313-5232 **Zero to Three National Center for Infants, Toddlers and Families** (800) 899-4301 **Starlight Children's Foundations** (800) 274-7827

Chapter 2
Parenting

Children are likely to live up to what you believe in them

Lady Bird Johnson

With the dynamics of parents changing with time, the need for stable, loving, and protective parents has not. Children rely on parents to be an example to teach them how to be independent self-sufficient human beings. The creativity and path belongs to each child. Parents expect children to be appreciative of their efforts and understanding of their limitations. The burden of responsible parenting lies with each adult.

☼How The Information Was Found

Parents can take comfort in knowing that help is available. Many resources are available to parents and children for nearly any given topic. Furthermore, hundreds of publishers have titles dedicated to parents and children.

The web research for this chapter went smoothly and it was good to know that most of the online resources remained current over the years.

Resources for specific types of families, such as Latin, Chinese, and African families were not in abundance, but the general topic of *families* results address all types.

It was a pleasant surprise to see the many grand parents and blended families web pages. Please keep up those beautiful web pages!

ABOUT PARENTING

Children need examples and exposure to assist with their spiritual, emotional, and academic growth. Parents, being the primary caretakers, are granted the privilege of influencing the lives their children. As this is a challenging experience wrought with ups and downs, it's also the single most rewarding privilege given to mankind. Parents face many obstacles while trying to maintain stability in the home (often times this is done without a partner). Children are continuously observing parents responses to different situations. As they observe your strength and calm during challenges of life, a child's thanks to parents is his/her unconditional love forever.

Legal Responsibilities of Parents

Parents are the legal custodians of their children. Parents are responsible for their overall care including but not limited to food, clothing, shelter, health (both physical and emotional), education, and safety.

Parenting is a serious matter as most of us children inevitably mimic our parent's behavior. Keeping control of your emotions when you correct children and finding creative solutions are difficult aspects to parenting. Both parents and children must laugh and smile together. Hold their young hands when they need your support and in time all that you invest is returned in unexpected ways and measures. As all children want to please their parents and all parents worry about their children. Relax – enjoy life together, as time is brief and only now.

Location	Source	
Books	Sheedy, Mary. *Raising Your Spirited Child Workbook.* New beginnings © 1999. Goldberg, Linda et al. *Pregnancy To Parenthood.* Leaven, © 2001.	
Web	www.abcparenting.com www.positiveparenting.com www.familiesusa.org	www.iwannaknow.org www.npin.org
Agencies	**American Social Health Association** P. O. Box 13827 Research Triangle Park, NC 27709-3827 (800) 783-9877 **Campaign For Our Children (CFOC)** 120 west Fayette St. Baltimore, MD 21201	**Families USA** 1334 G Street, NW Washington, DC 20005 (202) 628-3030

Parenting Classes

Part of planning for the arrival of a baby is preparing yourself with information that will help develop a strong functional relationship between you and your child. Parenting classes provide a solid foundation for you and your baby. Parenting teachers are a valuable resource for information and they can answer questions that anxious parent's may have. Knowledgeable instructors are able to link behavior patterns that have been passed on from previous generations in order to help you identify the source of any problem(s) and provide insightful information on how to correct issues. Considering that these behaviors could eventually be taught to your child, parenting class is a wise investment.

Location	Source
Web	www.positiveparenting.com www.momsonline.com www.parentingqa.com www.parentsplace.com www.npin.org www.abcparenting.com www.familyeducation.com/home/ www.twinstoday.com www.helpforfamiles.com/frameparent.htm
Agencies	**Mothers at Home** 8310 A Old Courthouse Rd. Vienna, VA 22182

Severing Parental Rights

Parental rights can be terminated by choice as in adoption or by a judge in cases of abandonment and/or neglect.

Abandonment/Neglect

Cases where physical and emotional abuse by a parent is evident, restoring parental rights is difficult. A parent can be criminally charged with abuse, including willful neglect and/or abandonment. The laws as to what constitutes abuse vary depending on the state where the incident occurs as well as the degree of the charge for abuse. In these matters it is important to retain the services of a competent attorney for clarification of the laws.

The general legal process for child abuse involves the child removal from the home typically by a police officer that more than likely received a call about abuse. The officer performs an initial interview with the child and later with the parent(s) or guardian. After the initial investigation, if the officer suspects abuse he contacts a social worker to perform an onsite assessment of the alleged abuse. An investigator later files a complaint with the local district attorney's office. The child is placed in either an emergency group or foster home until the judge, using his/her discretion, determines the next course of action, always keeping in mind the child's best interest. The judicial system becomes responsible for the minor's well being; a court hearing occurs within days of the reported incident. During the child's absence from the home, the courts often grant supervised visitation to one or both parents until a court ruling. If both biological parents are being charged with abuse, particularly sexual abuse, visitation is unlikely to be granted until the investigation is completed. *See also the section on Sexual/Physical Abuse in this chapter.*

The courts are careful to complete a thorough investigation before severing the parent-child relationship. When the state takes custody of a child experts are called upon to provide detailed reports from their interviews with the parent and child before stating their opinion to the court. Typically, multiple hearings occur before parental custody is restored.

When the person inflicting harm, to the child, resides in the same household, the courts often order that the [accused] abusive parent must vacate the home before custody is returned to the non-abusive parent.

Location	Source
Web	www.gocrc.com www.childensdefense.org www.usakids.org www.teenlit.com www.cwla.org www.childadvocacy.org www.advocateforyouth.org www.childadvocate.net
Agencies	**ABA Center For Children and Law** 750 15th Street, NW 9th Floor Washington, DC 20005-1022 (202) 662-1720 **Children's Rights Council** 6200 Editors Park Drive, Suite 103 Hyattsville, MD 20782 (301) 559-3120 **Child Welfare League of America** 440 First Street, NW Third Floor Washington, DC 20001	**Children's Defense Fund** 25 E Street, NW Washington, DC 20001 (202) 628-8787 **Advocates For Youth** 1025 Vermont Ave., NW Suite 200 Washington, DC 20005 (202) 347-5700 **Child Help USA National Abuse Hotline** 15757 N. 78th Street Scottsdale, AZ 85260 (800) 4-A-Child (800) 2-A-Child (TDD)

MEDICAL AND DENTAL NEEDS

Children are active and require lots of attention for establishing good hygiene and sound medical care. Certain health care practitioners specialize in treating children; for instance some dental practices are tailored to young children. Children that do have special medical needs, visits to pediatrician or medical care provider should occur as recommended by your professional practitioner. Parents should always accompany their child to the practitioner's office and remain present during examinations to obtain an understanding of your child's health and physical growth, and for safety precautions.

Location	Source	
Books	Dr. Schmidt, Michael A. *Healing Childhood Ear Infections: Prevention, Home Care and Alternative Treatment.* Leaven, © 1998. Sears, William MD and Martha Sears RN. *The Family Nutrition Book: Everything You Need To know About Feeding Your Children-From Birth Through Adolescence.* New Beginnings © 2000.	
Web	www.apsa.org www.aapd.org www.aap.org	www.kidshealth.org www.childrenshc.org www.drs4kids.com www.ichp.edu
Agencies	**Center/Improvement/ Childcare** 11331 Ventura Blvd, Suite 103 Studio City, CA 91604 (800) 325-2422 **American Academy of Pediatrics** 141 Northwest Point Blvd. Elks Grove Village, IL 60007-1098 (847) 434-4000	**Child Help USA/Hotline** 15757 N. 78th Street Scottsdale, AZ 85260 (800) 422-4453 (800) 4-A-CHILD **For Kids Sake** 24710 Washington St. Suite 5 Murrieta, CA 92562 (800) 898-4543

STEP-PARENTING

Most of us are familiar with television shows like *The Brady Bunch,* which depicted a blended family that had minor ups and downs but overall got along well with each other. After watching the show many children wanted half brothers and sisters. And there are movies like *Yours, Mines, Ours* that portrayed a more realistic blended family. Most of us didn't want to experience additions to our family after watching that movie (if you notice in both shows the other biological parent was not involved in the children's lives, which isn't reality for many stepparents). Step parenting is becoming commonplace in our society as the rise in divorces. One type of blended family doesn't exist each varies, as some children do not see one of the biological parents, are older and no longer minors, and/or have involved relationships with the non custodial biological parent. Nevertheless, help is available for stepparents who have taken on the challenge of blending their families.

Location	Source
Books	Fox, Kathleen. *Making The Best of Second Best.* Fox Craft Inc. © 1998. Visher, Emily and John. *How To Win As A Step Family.* Brunner / Mazel, © 2001. Zieghn, Suzen J. Ph.D. *7 Steps to Bonding with Your Step* Child. Griffen © 2001.
Web	www.stepfamily.net www.stepfamilyinfo.org www.stepmoms.net www.stepfam.org www.tsconnection.org

Location	Source	
Agencies	**Step Family Association of America** 650 J. Street, Suite 205 Lincoln, NE 68508 (800) 735-0329 **Family Madallion Clergy Services, Inc.** P.O. Box 32333 Kansas City, MO 64171	**Step Family Foundation** 333 West End Ave. New York, NY 10023 (212) 877-3244 (212) 799-STEP (Info Line)

SINGLE PARENTING

As the number of people choosing not to marry increases so does the increase in children born to single parents. Whether by choice or otherwise parenting is challenging when taken on by one-self. Single parents agree that they receive help from family members, friends, or hired caregivers to assist with the rearing of children. No matter how successful the parent he/she relies upon help. For those who are interested in becoming single parents or already have children there are many resources and support groups available.

Location	Source	
Web	www.single-parents.com www.parentswithoutpartners.org www.makinglemonade.com www.fatherhood.org www.singlefathers.org www.single-fathers.org www.parentworld.com	
Agencies	**Parents Without Partners** 401 N. Michigan Ave.	**Single Parent Association**

Location	Source
	Chicago, IL 6011-4267 (800) 704-2102
	(602) 788-5511
	Single Mothers by Choice
	200 E 84th Street
	New York, NY 10028

GRAND PARENTING

Nobody can do for children what grandparents do. Grandparents sort of sprinkle stardust over the lives of little children
Alex Haley

I like the phase *It takes a village to raise a child* because it does. Grandparents are essential family members and oftentimes prove vital to the guidance of children. I'm always jealous of the how my niece and nephew are lovingly treated by my mother, who provided my sisters and I with a stricter rearing. Grandparents have something special about them, which is priceless to both parents and children; they add another dimension to family history and pass on cultural distinctions that children need to strengthen their character. Many grandparents relish that when they're done visiting they simply send the child home. For grandparents who have taken on the responsibility of raising their grandchildren, and those who can send their little ones home, the following resources are provided.

Location	Source
Book	Truly, Traci. *Grandparents Rights 3rd Edition.* Sphinx Publishing © 2001.
	www.grandparentedge.com

Location	Source
Web	www.grandparenting.org
	www.grandparentworld.com
Agencies	**National Center On Poverty Law** 205 West Monroe Street Chicago, IL 60606 (312) 263-3830 (Provides Information on Grand Parenting Visitation) **The Foundation For Grand Parenting** 108 Farnham Road Ojai, CA 93023	**AAPR Grandparent Information Center** 601 E Street, NW Washington, DC 20049 (202) 434-2296 (800) 424-3410

FOSTER PARENTING

Foster parents are those who the court has appointed as guardian of a child. When biological parents are not capable of caring for their child the court, with the assistance of a social worker, selects a guardian, although the child remains the custody of the state. For thousands of children the only parent they know is their foster parent.

Foster parents were intended to only be temporary guardians of a minor. The foster parents have no legal rights to the child, as the state remains the custodial agent. Foster parents are paid by the state or certified agency to care for the child; they are to provide food, clothing, shelter as well as access to medical care and education. Foster parents are granted a restricted amount of decision-making rights by the court on a temporary basis until parental custody is restored, adoption occurs, or emancipation is granted. Children may remain in foster care for several years until the age of majority, reunified with family, or emancipation (for more information regarding emancipation see the following page). Many foster parents choose to adopt a child in their care (*for more information on adoption, refer to the Adoption section in this chapter*). Once the minor enters the foster home a social worker is assigned to follow up on the needs of the minor. Many of the following web sites have recommended books written by and for foster parents.

Location	Source	
Web	www.fostercarechildren.com http://fostercare.org/FPHP http://fostercare.org www.nfpainc.org www.cadvocates.org www.thejoyofraisingfosterchildren.com www.baprc.org/mainmenu.html	
Agencies	**National Foster Parent Association, Inc** 7512 Stanich Ave. #6 Gig Harbor, WA 98335 (253) 853-4000 (800) 557-5238 **Black Adoption Placement and Research Center** 125 Second Street Oakland, CA 94607 (800) 299-3678	**The Children's Aid Society** 105 East 22nd Street New York, NY 10010 (212) 949-4800 **Child Help USA** (877)-70-CHILD

Resources For Foster Children

Foster children also have rights and support groups available to provide assistance. The following resources are worth investigation for foster youth.

Location	Source	
Web	www.youthlaw.org www.fosterclub.com www.fostercarechildren.com www.childrensaidsociety.org www.factsupportgroup.com www.soschildrensvillages.org	
Agencies	**National Center For Youth Law** 405 14ᵗʰ Street, 15ᵗʰ Oakland, CA 94612-2701 (501) 835-8098 **Youth Communication/ NY Center, Inc.** 224 W. 29th St. New York, NY 10001 (212) 279-0708	**The Children's Aid Society** 105 East 22nd Street New York, NY 10010 (212) 949-4800

Emancipation

Emancipation occurs when the courts terminate their custodial relationship with a child. This can be done at the request of the minor on or before his/her 19th birth date (or the age of majority). At the age of 19 the courts automatically terminate their relationship, as the minor is the age of majority.

Many states offer emancipation programs for minors approaching the age of adulthood. The minor is enrolled by his/her social worker in a training course for learning skills pertinent for independent living. This includes basic skills such as learning how to obtain a job, budget income, obtain essential state identifications, purchase a vehicle, obtaining shelter (such as an apartment), apply for college, etc. Foster youths are made aware of special programs for foster children provided locally, statewide, and federally. If the minor will be attending college, applying for grants and loans available to the child is covered during this course.

ADOPTING CHILDREN

Adopted parents are those who have obtained complete guardianship of a child by a court of law. Adopted children are regarded the same as biological children in the eyes of the courts. Adopted children are the complete responsibility of the adoptive parent and are entitled to the same benefits as biological children.

Adopting a child is a wonderful choice. People who have a desire to adopt but are not sure of where to begin and what steps are involved with the process can seek information from the following resources. Many of the resources can assist persons wanting to adopt children with disabilities or without an attorney's service.

Location	Source
Web	www.adopting.org
	www.raisingadoptedchildren.com
	www.adoptionsearch.com
	www.adoptionhelp.org
	www.adoption.com
	www.adopt.net
	www.ncfa-usa.org
	www.calib.com/naic
	www.adoptionattorneys.org
	www.adoption.org
	www.adopt.org

Location	Source
	www.adopting.org www.adopt-USA.com www.baprc.org www.soschildrensvillages.org www.face2000.org www.ffpa.org
Agencies	**Bethany Christian Services** **National Headquarters** P.O. Box 294 Grand Rapids, MI 49501-0294 (800) 238-4269 **National Adoption Center** 1500 Walnut Street Suite 701 Philadelphia, PA 17102 (800) 862-3678 **SOS Children's Villages-USA** 1317 F Street, NW, Suite 550 Washington, DC 20004 (800) 886-5767 **International Christian** **Adoption** **Institute for Children's AID** 41745 Rider Way **Suite 2** Temecula, CA (909) 695-3336	**Black Adoption** **Placement** **and Research Center** 125 Second Street Oakland, CA 94607 (800) 299-3678 **Family Life Services** 124 Liberty Mountain Dr. P.O. Box 4199 Lynchburg, VA 24502 (800) 542-4453 **North American Council** **on Adoptive Children** 970 Raymond Ave. Suite 106 St. Paul, MN 55114-1149 **Families Adopting In** **Response (FAIR)** P.O. Box 51436 Palo Alto, CA 94303 (650) 856-3513

Support for Adopted Children

Adopted children are special in the eyes of their [adoptive] parents; likewise adoptive parents are extra sensitive to the emotions of adopted children. When children learn of their adoption support may be needed to provide assistance with understanding of their importance in the family. Several organizations and newsletters are designed to help adopted children.

Location	Source	
Web	www.helpforkids.com www.adoption-help.net www.adoptionquest.com	www.adopt-USA.com www.itslegal.com
Agencies	**Bethany Christian Services/National National Headquarters** P.O. BOX 294 Grad Rapids, MI 49501-0294 (800) 238-4269 **International Christian Adoption Institute for Children's AID** 41745 Rider Way, Suite 2 Temecula, CA (909) 695-33336 (909) 388-1753 **Family Life Services** 124 Liberty Mountain Dr. P.O. Box 4199 Lynchburg, VA 24502 (800) 542-4453	**National Council For Adoption** 1930 17th St. NW Washington, DC 20009 **National Adoption Center** 1500 Walnut Street Philadelphia, PA 19102 (800) 862-3678 (215) 735-9410

Locating a Biological Parent

Children who have been adopted will eventually want to know about their biological parents. If it was an open adoption, then oftentimes the [adopted] parent will have knowledge about the [biological] parents' whereabouts or at least a previous address to begin searching. For children who learn of their adoption as a minor locating a biological parent may require the consent of their parents. The following resources are available to those desiring to locate [biological] parents.

Location	Source	
Web	www.almasociety.com www.the-seeker.com/adoptees.htm www.bastards.org www.aborn.org	
Agencies	**ALMA Society (Adoptees' Liberty Movement Association)** P.O. Box 727 Radio City Station New York, NY 10101-0727 (212) 581-1568 **Adoptees and Birth Parents for Open Records Nationwide** Route 4 Box 361 Adrian Missouri 64720	**Voices of Adoption** 2006 22nd Avenue San Francisco, CA, 94116 (415) 759-9515

LOCATING CHILD CARE

Accessing quality childcare requires hours of interviewing candidates or sheer luck. The best resource for locating quality care is through referral. Knowledgeable workers are in demand and scarce. Before determining childcare consider the following:

- Decide if you want a live-in caregiver, or prefer to take your child to a center.
- How much money can you afford per week or month?
- Does your child require special needs? Include all the medications and health conditions that require attention.
- Do you have a responsible relative who is available during working hours, or someone who attends school at night and is able to watch your child during the day for extra money?
- Would you consider a childcare agency operated out of a house (private home day care)? Verify that the care agency is state certified and has proper insurances and licenses. Persons who have had professional experience with children is desirable.

Types of Childcare

Private Home Day Care

Home day care centers are rapidly increasing as many families find quality care from those who live within their community. Each state has laws and requirements for private home day care centers such as the safety of the home,

Some private day care centers are publicly funded, and are capable of offering free or significantly discounted childcare to qualified families. Ask the centers owner or intake representative for information.

number of children allowed to attend, and hours of operation. Verify with the State Department of Licensing to ensure that the home you select is currently licensed and has passed inspections.

The costs of home day care varies, as these are privately operated, call several locations before making a decision. When it comes to your child quality is key over cost. Prior to enrollment, verify their requirements for certain vaccinations, toilet training, language requirements or other special requests. If the home has a swimming pool, then ensure that it is properly fenced. Remember to use common sense when searching for day care facilities.

Location	Source	
Web	www.edaycare.com www.nncc.org	www.nccic.org www.trustline.org
Agencies	**State Department of Licensing** (800) 822-8490 **National Association Education of Young Children** 1509 16th Street, NW Washington, DC 20036 (800) 424-2460 (Provides a list of Accredited Child Care Centers)	**National Child Care Information Center (NCCIC)** 243 Church Street, NW 2nd Floor Vienna, Virginia 22180 (800) 616-2242 (800) 516-2242 (TTY)

Day Care Centers

We all have seen mini vans transporting children of all ages driving into shopping center parking lots where they spend hours until their parent's arrival. Most day care centers are privately owned or franchised by private parties to care for children of various ages. Similarly to private home day care, these establishments must be licensed and provide services to a set number of children. These centers typically have trained staff and volunteers employed. Verify with the day care center manager or owner as to how many staff have college degrees or are in the process of *completing* a degree related to the care of children. The following resources provide information for selecting and locating *quality* day care center:

Location	Source	
Web	www.nncc.org www.nccic.org	www.edaycare.com www.careguide.com
Agencies	**State Department of Licensing** (800) 822-8490 **National Association for the Education of Young Children** 1509 16th Street, NW Washington, DC 20036 (800) 424-2460 (Provides Lists of accredited child care centers)	**The Child Care Bureau U.S. Department of Health and Human Services Administration of Children, Youth and Families Child Care Bureau** Switzer Building Room 2046 330 C Street, SW Washington, DC 20447 (202) 690-6782 **National Child Care Information Center (NCCIC)**

Location	Source
	243 Church Street, NW 2nd Floor Vienna, Virginia 22180 (800) 616-2242 (800) 516-2242 (TTY)

Nannies and Babysitters

Nannies are live in care givers that provide child care assistance to families. Typically they receive pay (or pocket money) plus room and board. Nannies perform light household chores such as preparing meals, cleaning, laundry, as well as a host of other child supportive services for the family; they have a commitment to a family for at least one year.

The local high school or college may prove an excellent source for locating a babysitter. Many schools interview candidates and verify their reliability and temperament by obtaining references from teachers and faculty. Students under the legal working age can obtain a work permit as long as the hours are within the legal limit.

Babysitters provide similar services as nannies, however, babysitters do not take residence in the home and they work for a limited amount of hours and days. Agencies are available to assist families with the selection of a nanny or babysitter - both are trained to stay with the child without parental supervision.

Location	Source
Web	www.babiestoday.com www.edaycare.com www.careguide.com

Au Pair

Au Pairs are similar to nannies as they typically take up residence in the family home; they work for families for a limited time, typically one year. Their services are provided within or outside their country of origin. Customarily they are part of a family for no more than one year. Like nannies they perform light household chores, given a room and are provided pocket money. Some au pairs are not trained to remain with children without parental supervision, although families, who have grown to trust their au pair, often leave their children alone with the caregiver.

Location	Source
Web	www.iapa.org www.aupairinamerica.com www.au-pair-box.com www.edaycare.com
Agencies	**International Au Pairs Association (IAPA)** Bredgade 25 H • DK-1260 Copenhagen K, Denmark 45- 3333- 9600 **Au Pair in America** River Plaza 9 West Broad Street Stamford, CT 06902 (800) 928-7247

Children Programs

After school programs are mutually beneficial to parents, children, and the community. Programs such as boy scouts and girl scouts provide children and their parents an opportunity to explore their surrounding community as well as learn new crafts and skills. Sport programs and science clubs are a few examples of activities available to children. The success of your child and the program is dependant upon involved parents.

Location	Source	
Web	www.youthlink.org www.gsusa.org www.shine.com www.childnet.org www.ymca.net www.ywca.org www.bgca.org	www.ctitykids.com www.littleleague.org www.bsa.scouting.org www.edaycare.com www.girlscouts.org
Agencies	**Boy Scouts of America** P.O. Box 152079 Irving, TX 75015-2079 **YWCA USA** Empire State Building 350 Fifth Ave, Suite 301 New York, NY 10118 (212) 273-7800 **SHiNE** 427 Broadway Suite 41 New York, NY 10013 (646) 613-5100 (877) SHiNE-65	**Girl Scouts USA** 420 Fifth Avenue New York, NY 10018-2798 (800) GSUSA 4 U (800) 478-7248 **YMCA USA** 101 North Wacker Dr. Chicago, IL 60606 (312) 977-0031

RESOURCES FOR LOW-INCOME PARENTS

Children of all economic backgrounds have similar needs. Parents with little or no money may find that supporting the needs of their child[ren] is difficult. Taking advantage of the free or discounted programs available may assist parents with paying for daily needs. Many of the resources offered by the state and federal government offer free or low cost services to family on restricted budget.

Location	Source
Web	www.povertylaw.org www.catholiccharitiesusa.org www.childrennow.org www.healthykidsproject.org www.childrendefense.org www.nbcdi.org
Agencies	**Catholic Charities USA** 1731 King Street, Suite 200 Alexandria, VA 22314 **National Center on Poverty Law, Inc.** 205 West Monroe Street Chicago, IL 60606 (312) 263-3830

DEATH OF CHILDREN

The loss of a child is devastating to love ones, especially when the loss is unexpected. Children are an extension of our own lives—a way of living forever. The impact of their presence is never forgotten. You can heal from this loss without losing your own life to their passing. Yes, healing is possible eventhough your life is altered and reshaped.

Some parents take the experience of losing a child and create organizations to help others who have lost children under similar circumstances. Some find solace in creating memory stones, writing books, paintings, quilting, or other crafts that are permanent memories of their love for the child. Begin

 For information on children hospice Programs refer to the Hospice Care section in Chapter 15.

healing by taking some action and talking. Talk with people who listen with an open heart as you continue to mend. Do not feel rushed to heal; take your time. Support from family and friends are vital; although it is understandable to be alone and not want to discuss your feelings until you have an understanding of what has happened. When it is time integrate back into your life, do it slowly but certainly strive to regain yourself. Additional resources are located in the Chapter 15, Death and Dying.

Location	Source	
Web	www.bereavedparentsUSA.org www.compassionatefriends.org www.alivealone.org www.pomc.com www.missfoundation.org www.twinlesstwin.org www.agast.org	
Agencies	**Compassionate Friends** P.O. Box 3696 Oak Brook, IL. 60522-3696 (630) 990-0010 **Alliance of Grandparents, A Support in Tragedy**	**Alive Alone** c/o Kay Bevington 11115 Dull Robinson Rd Van Wert, OH 45891 **Bereaved Parents of**

Location	Source	
	(AGAST)	**the USA**
	P.O. Box 17281	P.O. Box 95
	Phoenix, AZ 85011-0281	Park Forest, IL 60466
	(888) 774-7437	
	National Organization of Parents of Murdered Children	
	100 East Eighth Street, Suite B-41	
	Cincinnati, Ohio 45202	
	(513) 721-5683	

DISABLED CHILDREN

Disabilities are placed into two main categories: physical and mental disability. Vast numbers of classifications exist for the types of problems a person may have. For each type of disability resources are available for both children and parents. Because there is such a vast amount of conditions classified as disabilities it is difficult to list all of the applicable resources. To find more information, contact local schools, you may need to call more than one, for information on resources for disabled children. A diligent worker will help you research the condition and locate specific resources. The medical professional that diagnosed the problem should refer the family to a specialist who is familiar with the condition; he/she can provide resources. Seek additional opinions from other practitioners as this may prove to be of great assistance. *See chapter 3 for information on disabled children in the school environment.*

Location	Source	
Books	Schiff, Donald. et.al. *American Academy of Pediatrics: The Official, Complete Home Reference Guide to Your Child's Symptoms.* Villard Books. © 1997. Schmitt, Barton D. *Your Child's Health: The Parent's Guide to Symptoms, Emergencies, Common Illnesses, Behavior and School Problems.* Bantam Books. © 1991.	Sears, William, MD and Martha Sears, RN. *The Fussy Baby: How To Bring The Best In Your High-Need Baby.* La Leche League International © 2000.
Web	www.blindkids.org www.ablelink.org www.aidskids.org www.deafnation.com www.childrenwithdisabilities.ncjrs.org www.deafzone.com www.aability.com www.navh.org www.nad.org www.aed.org www.amp-info.net	
Agencies	**Children with AIDS Project America** P.O. Box 23778 Tempe AZ 85285-3778 (480) 774-9718 (602) 973-4319 **ALS Association (Lou Gehrig's Disease)** 27001 Agoura Rd.	**National Association of the Deaf** **American Council of the Blind** 1155 15th St. NW Suite 1004 Washington, DC 20005 (800) 424-8666 **American Foundation for the Blind** 1 Penn Plaza Suite 300

Location	Source
Suite 180 Calabasas Hills, CA 91301-5104\ (800) 782-4747 **American Action Fund for the Blind** 18440 Oxnard St. Tarzana, CA 91356 **National Information Center for Youth with Disabilities** P.O. Box 1492 Washington, DC 20013 (800) 695-0285 **Beach Cities Braille Guild, Inc.** P. O. Box 112 Huntington Beach, CA 92648	New York, NY 10001 (800) 232-5463 **American Speech Language/Hearing** (ASHA) 10801 Rockville Pike Rockville, MD 20852 (800) 498-2071 **American Council of the Blind** 1155 15th St., NW., Suite 1004 Washington, DC 20005 (800) 424-8666 **Allergy and Asthma Network** **Mother's of Asthmatics, Inc** 2751 Prosperity Ave., Suite 150 Fairfax, VA 22031-4397 (800) 878-4403

Learning Disabled

Learning disabilities are often not discovered until children are measured against their peers. For more information on Learning Disabilities see the *Children With Disabilities* section in Chapter 3.

Mentally Handicap

Families who care for children with mental disabilities require help and must demand assistance. Many youngsters are incorrectly diagnosed, which prolongs their recovery and remedies. Have the correct diagnosis is significant to appropriately treat the child. Children with mental disabilities are often forgotten and neglected, so it is imperative to support families who need help.

Location	Source	
Web	www.nimh.nih.gov www.mentalhealth.org www.mentalhealth.net www.mentalwellness.com www.dr-bob.org www.nami.org www.mentalhealth.com www.coping.org	
Agencies	**National Institute of Mental Health** 6601 Executive Blvd. Room 8184, MSC 9663 Bethesda, MD 20892-9663 (301) 443-4513 (301) 443-8431(TTY) **National Alliance for the Mentally Ill Knowledge Exchange Network** Colonial Place Three 2107 Wilson Blvd., Suite 300 Arlington, VA 22201 (800) 950-6264 **Center For Mental Health Services** P. O. Box 42490 Washington, DC 20015 (800) 789-2647	**Depression Awareness** (800) 421-4211 **Brown Schools Information Research Services** P.O. Box 4008 Austin, TX 78765 (800) 531-5305 **National Referral Center** 222 W. Ball Rd. Anaheim, CA 92805 (800) 550-0467 **National Alliance for the Mentally Ill** 2107 Wilson Blvd. 3rd Floor

Location	Source	
	(866) 889-2647(TDD)	Arlington, VA 22201
		(800) 950-6264
	National Family Support	
	of the Mentally Ill	
	(800) 628-1696	

Physically Handicapped

The following resources range from poor eye sight to amputations. Depending on the condition, the help and resources vary, but do take comfort that help is available. Some organizations provide corrective lenses free of charge to selected families and there are organizations that assist families who have children suffering from viruses, cancers, and total disablement. Physicians/practitioners, school counselors, and elected officials have staff available to assist persons needing information about specific programs.

Location	Source	
Web	www.kidsneeds.com	www.amp-info.net
	www.kidscamp.com	www.wapd.org
Agencies	**Asthma Info. & Referral Line**	**World Association of Persons with Disabilities**
	(800) 822-2762	4503 Sunnyview Dr.,
		Suite 1121
	National Library Services for the Blind and Physically Handicapped	Oklahoma City, OK 73135
	C/O Library of Congress	(405) 672-4440

Location	Source
	Washington, DC 20542
	(800) 424-8567

PROBLEMS AT HOME

Both parents and children have their own personalities. The little infant who you held and fed will one day learn to speak to voice his or her viewpoints that will eventually contradict your parental perspective. Before children learn to speak they exhibit individuality just as parents did when they were the same age. Effectively guiding children requires consistency in seeing life from their perspective and comparing that to your experience. Even with the best intentions, problems do occur. Mitigating the issues so that they do not hinder the parent-child and sibling relationships requires the benefit of experience with problem solving. For parents who have multiple children, refereeing insignificant issues can be tiresome, but that is how children learn; they follow your examples in problem solving to remedy their own discrepancies. For both parents and children help is available.

Location	Source
Books	Moran, Victoria. *Shelter For The Spirit: How To Make Your Home a Haven in a Hectic World. New Beginning,* © 1998. Miller, Timothy PhD. *Wanting What You Have.* Publisher Group West, ©1998.
Web	www.familyeducation.com www.boystown.org www.wholefamily.com www.thefamily.com

Location	Source	
	www.talkingwithkids.org www.iparenting.com www.helpforfamlies.com www.mom.com www.bolt.com	
Agencies	**National Association Anorexia Nervosa & Associated Disorders (ANAD)** P.O. Box 7 Highland Park, IL. 60035 (847) 831-3438	**Over Eaters Anonymous** 6075 Zenith Court NE P.O. Box 44020 Rio Rancho, NM 87174-4020 (505) 891-2664
	Girls and Boys Town National Hotline (800) 448-3000 (800) 448-1833 (TDD) **Hit Home Youth Crisis Hot Line** (800) 448-4663 (800) HIT-HOME	**Boys Town National Hotline** (800) 448-3000 (Crises Hotline for Children & Parents) **Girls and Boys Town** 14100 Crawford Street Boys Town, NE 68010 (402) 498-1072 (800) 448-3000

Sexual/Physical Abuse

A principal component of parenting is protecting children. Parents must maintain an open dialog with their children as predators look for children who are ignored by their parents. Children who have suffered the humiliation and shame from being sexually and/or physically abused desperately need help. The following are a few resources:

Location	Source
Web	www.childnet.net www.missingkids.org www.foryourhealing.com http://www.child.cornell.edu
Agencies	**National Center for Missing and Exploited Children** 699 Prince Street Alexandria, VA 22314 703-274-3900 (800) THE-LOST **Rape, Abuse and Incest National Network** 252 Tenth Street, NE Washington, DC 20002 (800) 656-Hope (800) 843-5678 (800) 826-7653 (TDD) **National Foundation for Abused and Neglected Children** P.O. Box 608143 Chicago, IL 60660-8134 **Covent House NINE LINE** (800) 999-9999 **Rape, Abuse, and Incest Network (RAIN)** (800) 656-4673 **Behavioral Health Services** 15519 Crenshaw Blvd. Gardena, CA 90249 **National Referral Center** 222 W. Ball Road Anaheim, CA 92805 (800) 550-0467 **Child Help National Child Abuse Hotline** (800) 422-4453 **Child-Help USA** (800) 4-A-Child (800) 2-A-Child (TDD)

Substance Abuse

Help is available for children who have begun abusing substances. Many schools offer intervention programs to help children who have begun substance abuse. Parents often find that substance use is a hideaway for other problems. Seeking help from a licensed professional is essential during such times. Depending on your relationship, if both parent and child communicate openly, the solution can be found within your home.

Location	Source	
Web	www.additionresourceguide.com www.quitsmokingsupport.com www.alcoholics-anonymous.org www.12steps.com www.addictions.net www.well.com www.samhsa.org	
Agencies	**GRADS** P.O. BOX 27437 San Diego, CA 92198-1437 (858) 452-8152 **(800) Relapse** (800) 735-2773 (Information and Referral) **(888) Marijuana** (888) 627-4582 (Information and Referral) **Alcohol 24 Hour Help Line** (800) 252-6465 (Information and Referral) **National Youth Crises Hotline**	**National Association Children Alcoholics** 11426 Rockville Pike, Suite 100 Rockville, MD 20852 (888) 554-2627 **National Referral Center** 222 W. Ball Road Anaheim, CA 92805 **Cast Center for Substance Abuse** Treatment (800) 622-4357 **National Council on Alcohol & Drug** Dependency (800) 622-2255 **(800) 9Herion** (800) 943-7646

Location	Source
	(800) 448-4663 (Information Referral and Hotline)

Substance Abuse and Mential Health Services Administration Department of Health and Human Services
5600 Fisher lane
Rockville, MD 20857
(800) 729-6686
(800) 487-4889 (TTY)

(800) Cocaine
(800) 262-2463
(Information and Referral)

Be Sober Hotline
(800) 237-6237
(800) Be-Sober
(Referral Service)
(800) 345-2747 (Crisis Number)

Matrix Institute on Addictions
(800) 991-3784
(800) 991-DRUG
Information and Referral Services

Alcohol and Drug Help line
(800) 821-4357

AD CARE Hospital Help line
(800) ALCOHOL

Chapter 3

Education (Head Start - 12th grade)

*A pupil from whom nothing is ever
demanded which he cannot do never does
all he can*

John Stuart Mill

E ducation is a continuing process that begins at conception. Children learn and evolve all throughout their lives. Programs such as preschool and head start are designed to prepare children with a solid academic begining. With many options available parents can choose the best resource for their children's educational and emotional success.

☼How The Information Was Found

Information about home schooling was located. An article form an online broadcast station regarding the success of children who receive home schooling was used as a starting point for my research; they listed many links, which was researched further to obtain some of the information contained in this chapter.

The Waldorf School information was obtained online by sheer luck (several links on a web page appeared while searching for information on boarding schools, by accident I clicked on a link). Their philosophy is refreshing and impressive. The links are contained in this chapter for your reference.

The college prep school information and boarding school resources are clearly accessible on the web. Books that provide additional insight are also listed.

EDUCATION OPTIONS

No longer do parents need to rely on traditional public schools to educate their children. With many alternatives available parents can select from a variety of options at economical costs to ensure that children receive the best education possible, even if they do it

GED Hotline
P.O. Box 81826
Lincoln, NE 68501
(800) 626-9433
(800) 62 My GED

themselves. A few options are covered in this chapter but finding more information is a click away via the Internet.

Public schools

Public schools are the most economical option available to parents for educating their children. Public schools receive funding from city, county, state, federal, and private grants. The curriculum varies depending on the school and district. One school district may excel in academics and another can fail miserably although both are within the same vicinity. Parents also have an option to send their children to public preparatory and magnet schools that provide focused leaning in mathematics, science, and/or music. Inquire about magnet schools from local school counselors.

Location	Source
Web	www.publiceducation.org www.asd.com www.caughtinthemiddle.org www.nea.org
Agencies	**National Education Association** 1201 16th Street, NW Washington, DC 20036-3290 (202) 833-4000 **GED Hotline** P.O. Box 81826 Lincoln, NE 68501 (800) 626-9433 (800) 62-MYGED

Voucher Programs

Voucher programs are great for parents who desire to remove their child from a public school located in one region and to another school (private or public). Voucher programs have received a great amount attention during the past two years. The topic of the last election and primaries included whether the government should sponsor voucher programs. Now that these programs are available parents can take time to evaluate their options.

Types Private Schools

Private schools vary according to the costs and curriculum. Many private schools offer tuition, vouchers, and grants to families for supplementing the cost of attendence. The following sections are types of private schools available for parents to research:

Montessori School

Maria Montessori developed the Montessori method based on the premise that each child is born with a drive to develop, discover, explore, and create in an enriched environment with supportive encouragement. The unique Montessori materials are self-directed to activate a desire in children to learn more, by engaging children both physically and mentally. Montessori schools may or may not be religious based.

Location	Source	
Web	www.montessori.org www.thematerialscompany.com www.amshq.org	
Agencies	**International Montessori Society** 912 Thayer Avenue #207 Silver Spring, MD 20910 (301) 589-1127 **The Montessori Foundation** 5948 Myakka Valley Trail Sarasota, FL 34241 (941) 927-9327	**American Montessori Society** 2020 E. Randol Mill Road Suite 307 Arlington, TX 76011 (817) 277-7791

College preparatory schools

College preparatory schools focus on teaching children based on the curriculum of many college courses. College preparatory courses are stringent to meet the requirements of colleges. The fast paced pressured learning environment is not for all children. Parents must become involved with their child's learning program to ensure overall success, even if it requires removal from the program. Check with school counselors to learn more about their agreement with local colleges allowing high school students enroll in college level courses. These agreements are also referred to as flexible campus or dual enrollment programs. Some high schools will give high school course credit for college courses.

Location	Source	
Web	www.students-online.org www.petersons.com www.cathlolic.org www.boysschoolscoalition.org www.parachail.com www.vsg.edu.au www.schools.com	
Agencies	**National Coalition of Girls Schools** 57 main Street Concord, Mass. 01742 (978) 287-4485 **International Boys' Schools Coalition** PO Box 117 Dennis, MA 02638 (508) 385-4563	**The Association of Boarding Schools** 4455 Connecticut Avenue, Suite A-200 Washington, D.C. 20008 Phone: (202) 966-8705 (800) 541-5908

Military and Boarding schools

Military and boarding schools offer discipline, quality education, and independent skills that provide a successful beginning for young adults. Both military and boarding schools are located throughout the country and world. The Association of Boarding Schools, listed below is a great resource for interested persons.

Location	Source	
Web	www.ncgs.org www.jbsa.org www.wbsa.net www.schools.com/directory	www.mwbs.org www.isanne.org www.aisne.org
Agencies	**Independent Schools Association of Northern New England** (ISANNE) 5 Great Hill Court Erefer, NH (603) 775-7782 **The Association of Boarding Schools** 4455 Connecticut Avenue, Suite A-200 Washington, D.C. 20008 Phone: (202) 966-8705 (800) 541-5908	**Mid West Boarding Schools Administration Office** P.O. Box 218 Faribault, MN 55021 (800) 799-6927

Waldorf Schools

A Waldorf education is a unique and distinctive approach to educating children. Their system of doing away with the need for competitive testing and grading is certainly worth exploring for children who find tradition school structures intimidating. Waldorf schools have no central governing body, however there is an abundance of material for parents to read and various web sites provided below (also, they have material available to parents who desire to home school children using the Waldorf method).

Location	Source
Web	www.waldorflibrary.org www.thewaldorfschool.org www.bobnancy.com www.waldorf.net www.awsna.org
Agencies	**The Waldorf School** 739 Massachusetts Avenue Lexington, MA 02420 (781) 863-1062 **The Association of Waldorf Schools North America** 3911 Bannister Road Fair Oaks, CA 95628 (916) 961-0927

Home schools

Home schooling is becoming increasingly popular and it is proving to be a successful method of rearing children. Many spelling, and national geographic champions of late have been home schooled. Parents who home school their children are not necessarily wealthy; they often sacrifice to live on one income; however there are cost savings involved with teaching children at home, no need for costly uniforms, trendy cloths, or transportation. The decision to home school is not necessarily based on a religious belief. Various reasons or influences have turned many households into schools. Parents who home school have a network of resources available.

Location	Source
Books	Griffin, Mary. *The Home Schooling Handbook.* Leaven, © 1998.
Web	www.home-school.com www.absoluteauthority.com/homeschooling www.theideabox.com www.unschooling.com www.tecahinghome.com www.homes-cool.com www.home-ed-magazine.com
Agencies	**National Home Education Network** P. O. Box 7844 Long Beach, CA 90807 (518) 891-4714 (512) 345-4895 (503) 647-2992

HEAD START AND PRESCHOOLS

Head start is a nationally government-funded program for children between the ages of three and five years old. The programs are geared to providing an excellent academic start for children; they provide immunizations (or locations where immunizations are provided), family support services, and health screenings in addition to an early academic beginning.

The program is government funded, to allow participation for all people regardless of race; they have a zero tolerance for discrimination.

Location	Source
Web	www.earlychildhood.com www.familyeducation.com www.kidsource.com www.theideabox.com www.nncc.org www.zerotothree.org
Agencies	**National Center for Infants, Toddlers and Families** 734 15th St., NW Suite 1000 Washington, D.C. 20005 (202) 638-1144 E-mail: 0to3@zerotothree.org

PROBLEMS AT SCHOOL

Numerous reasons are given why children are not getting along at school. Teachers, coursework, student and faculty can contribute their unhappiness of a determined student. Children who have moved around in past years may find it difficult to *fit in* at school. Sometimes problems exist with other students who can be cruel and intimidating. Yet not all problems are directly correlated with others behavior. Children can experience problems at school when there are issues occurring in the home. Trained school counselors as well as parents can work together to assist the child during their difficulties by identifying and working through the student issues so that their focus returns to academics and healthy relationships and away from the problems. The following sections offer resources to parents and children

Problems with Peers

When children transfer their anger to other students, it can be dangerous to a child's physical well-being and esteem. Parents must pay close attention to complaints children express about peers. Although it is often harmless, one cannot predict the extent of the other child's hostility. Bullies on campus brutalize some children and deter them from progressing academically – this is harassment. Parents and students must notify teachers, counselors, and principals of children who behave in this manner.

Location	Source
Web	www.teentalk.com www.bolt.com www.ipl.org www.ed.gov
Agencies	**Family Policy Compliance Office** **U.S. Department of Education** 600 Independence Ave., SW Washington, DC 20202-4605 (202) 260-3887

Parents may find that removing their child from an unhealthy classroom environment may alleviate some concerns for children. Some teachers have more experience and exposure to children with various personalities and their talent may further a child's academic success.

Discrimination

Discrimination on school campuses is not uncommon. Teachers and faculty may bring their personal biases to work, which can negatively affect children of all races.

Parents must participate by meeting teachers and staff prior to agreeing to have your child placed in their classroom. If you feel that your child has been discriminated against, then contact the school principal and school board in writing (send the letter certified mail). Request that your child be immediately removed from the environment and that an alternative be provided that does not hinder your child's academics. Like employers, the law prohibits teachers or faculty from retaliating against children who file complaints of discrimination; see the following resources for more information:

Location	Source
Web	www.crin.org www.GYAD.net www.ed.gov/ocr www.mentalhealth.org/stigma
Agencies	**U.S. Department of Education** **Office for Civil Rights** Customer Service Team Mary E. Switzer Building 330 C Street, SW Washington, D.C. 20202 (800) 421-3481 TTY: (877) 521-2172 **Addressing Discrimination and Stigma** **Resource Center** (for person with mental illness) 1-800-540-0320

Retaining Children

Child retention (mostly used by public schools) is a proposed solution by teachers, principals, and school counselors for children who have not progressed academically as their peers in the same grade. States offer alternatives to children who are experiencing difficulty with certain subject matters such as IE (Individualized Education Plan) programs that allow children to receive special help in certain subject matters. For example, if a child is reading below grade level but performing at or beyond grade level in other subjects the solution may be to provide tutoring or reading lab time for the student while the other classmates remain in the classroom during reading time as an effort to provide help in the lacking area(s).

It is important to note that each states requirements for child retention varies. Review the state and, if applicable, county laws. Retention is the last resort and not the first option. The teacher, principal, and school counselor must demonstrate to the parent that every effort has been made to prevent retention and that they have complied with state and local regulations. In addition, they must demonstrate that enough time has been allotted between every intervention, to raise the child's skills to meet that of his/her peers.

When an academic problem has been identified, parents must be notified and included in the plans to assist the student prior to retaining the child.

In addition, consider schools whose curriculum is targeted towards assisting children similar to yours, for more information read the section on private schooling located in this chapter.

If the student has a documented disability (learning, physical, or mental), which requires special consideration, the decision to retain is based solely or that child inability to meet their individual goals. The goals are established by a panel of school administrators, and should not be compared with other students, as your child's needs are specific to him/her.

Suspending, Disciplining, and Expelling Children

The resources for this section have been combined, and appear at the end of this section.

Suspension

Suspension of a student typically occurs when the student has violated a school policy. The action could have occurred once or multiple times to warrant the suspension. Schools have adopted polices against harassment, drug possession, weapons, profanity, absences (which is counter productive to suspend a child for not attending school), clothing and a host of others. The school board determines these policies, and it is wise for parents to attend school board meeting to influence the outcome of these rules.

Parents are immediately notified when their child is suspended. The school typically provides resources to parents to assist with correcting offensive and dangerous behaviors. (During their suspension, students are required to complete class work to ensure that the student is not behind when returned to the traditional classroom environment)

Parents may need to request resources for help with behavior problems or make an appointment to speak with the principal or school board superintendent for assistance.

Students who are suspended from schools have the option to enroll in another school outside of the district or an alternative school as options to avoid the embarrassment of suspension.

Disciplining (Physically) Children at School

Physically disciplining children is an antiquated method correction as it damages the esteem of the child. If physical disciplining exists at your child's school, you along with other parents can unite to stop this form of corporal punishment. For parents who do not want their child struck, notify school officials, <u>IN WRITING</u>, explicitly stating that you do not want this for your child and request notification before disciplinary action is taken. The web links provided at the end of this section offer additional information and books for recommended reading for both school and at-home disciplining.

Expelling

Similar to suspensions, expulsions occur when it is found that a child has committed a gross violation of a school policy. Expulsions occur at the school board level because it is a permanent removal from the school district. Appeal to the local school board can overturn expulsions. Parents should be immediately notified of the act committed.

Obtain copies of the school, district, and state policies pertaining to expelling students along with your child's school records. Copies include all documentation in his /her file including notes scribbled on the folder. This should be provided to you at least two weeks prior to the hearing. Receiving documentation the same day or the day of the hearing doesn't provide enough time for review and therefore you are at a disadvantage for the meeting. Request a hearing for a later date in order to review the material. You want to ensure that the school

Public schools are considered federal property and receive federal, state, and local monies for operation. The federal laws prohibit discrimination of any sort.

followed their own policies and the state's policies. If they did not, then outline all the discrepancies and present them when you appear before the school board. In addition, the school can use discretion as to when it will suspend a student. For instance, a student may not be expelled for repeatedly wearing a T-shirt with profanity although the rule states this is cause for expulsion. Verify that the school board applies the rules equally to all students. This requires research. However, if you participate in the PTA and attend school board meetings, obtaining this information is not difficult.

Discrimination as to how expulsions are implemented is cause for legal inquiry. Speak with other parents and listen to your children who often provide valuable insight about the schools treatment of students who resemble them.

Location	Source	
Web	www.stophitting.com www.nopaddle.com www.NeverHitAChild.ORG www.nospank.net www.wrightslaw.com/info/discipl.gameplan.htm www.ncl.american.edu/journal/lawyer/so/insley.gif www.wcl.american.edu/journal/lawrev/50/insley.pdf www.ncte.org/action/edreports/5-10-02.shtml	
Agencies	**Center for Effective Discipline** 155 W. Main St. #1603 Columbus, Ohio 43215 Tel: (614) 221-8829 **The Natural Child Project** P.O. Box 3183 Sunriver, OR 97707	**Project NoSpank** Parents and Teachers Against Violence in Education (PTAVE). P.O. Box 1033, Alamo, CA 94507-7033 Telephone: (925) 831-1661

CHILDREN WITH DISABILITIES

Children with physical, mental and learning disabilities have many resources available to encourage their academic success. Public schools have trained staff on hand to guide children along the best path. Schools are no longer permitted to segregate children who have disabilities; every effort must be made to *mainstrea"* disabled children to avoid discrimination based on disability. Parents must participate in the plan, by becoming knowledgeable about their child's condition, diagnosed by a licensed practitioner and not the school nurse, to ensure that their child is not placed in an isolated area with little or no interaction with his/her peers. Parents can object to the schools plan, as true of a parent who sued the school district after they insisted that her child take[3]Ritalin. In addition, there are some schools that isolate children allowing them only to participate in recess with their peers but leave them unattended for hours in remote classrooms. Parents are the key to their child's success, and involvement is mandatory, especially with disabled children who are often neglected.

Location	Source	
Web	www.wrightslaw.com	www.thearc.org
	www.upca.org	www.addhelp.com
	www.downsyndrome.com	www.dishes.org
	www.cec.sped.org	www.amp-info.net
	www.irsc.org	www.conductdisorders.com
	www.npnd.org	www.autism.org
Agencies	**The Council For Exceptional Children**	**United Cerebral Palsy** 1600 L Street, NW

[5]Ritalin is a drug that has caused controversy as it is commonly prescribed to children who have been diagnosed as having Attention Deficit Disorder (ADD). Side effects have been known to kill certain children.

Location	Source
	1110 North Glebe Road Suite 300 Arlington, VA 22201-5704 (888) CEC-SPED (703) 264-9446 (TTY) **National Cristina Foundation** 500 West Putnam Greenwich, CT 06830 (203) 863-9100 **The Arc of the United State** 1010 Wayne Ave., Suite 650 Silver Springs, MD 20910 (301) 565-3842	Suite 700 Washington, DC 20036 **National Information Center for Children and Youth with Disabilities** P.O. Box 1492 Washington, DC 20013-1492 (800) 695-0285

PARENTAL INVOLVEMENT

Children rely on parents to be well informed and to take action on their behalf. Parents must pay close attention to their children to make certain their needs are being met. With single parenting on the rise and the increase of two-income households parents depend on schools to act responsibly. Schools are becoming even more overcrowded, plagued with century old problems, and lack of resources, which often leads to disappointed parents and students.

-ʘ- The Parent and Teacher Association (PTA) is a reputable organization that combines information and resources from both parents and teachers; they often meet on the school campus during non-working hours, for parents who work the hours may be convenient for your schedule. The PTA is always looking for enthusiastic parents.

Periodic Unannounced Visits

Once a group of parents opened a class action lawsuit against the school district for isolating their children by placing them in a lunchroom during classroom hours. Certain children were selected to stay in the lunchroom while the other children learned in the classroom; interestingly the children in the lunchroom were the same race. A parent noticed this occurrence and gathered the other parents in order to sue. It shouldn't take a lawsuit for parents to participate in their child's education, or for schools to recognize discrimination.

It is the right of parents to make periodic unannounced visits to the campus and classroom where your child attends (many schools will try to notify the teacher before your arrival). Parents are often times amazed at or impressed by their child's education environment. Take time during your lunch break or days off to stop by your child's school!

Location	Source
Books	Coburn, Kevin Levin and Madge Lawrence. *Letting Go: A Parents' Guide to Understanding the College Year.* Leaven, © 1999.

Location	Source
Web	www.kidsvista.com www.mrdowling.com www.awesomelibrary.org http://artsedge.kennedy-center.org www.pta.org www.act.org www.ala.org www.goals.com www.kidsbank.com www.caughtinthemiddle.org www.edgate.com
Agency	**American Library Association** 50 East Huron Chicago, IL 60611 (800) 545-2433 (888) 814-7692 (TTY)

ADDITIONAL INFORMATION

The following resources provide additional resource to parents and children.

Location	Source
Web	www.ed.gov/offices/ope/accrediation www.homeworkspot.com www.theschoolreport.com www.schoolmatch.com www.chea.org
Agency	**Upward Bound** Division of Student Services Education Outreach Branch Office of Post Secondary Education US Department of Education

Location	Source
	600 Independence Ave., SW
	Room 5065
	Washington, DC 20202
	(202) 260-1494

Chapter 4

Education (Colleges/ Universities and Specialized Schools)

There are two kinds of graduates; those who have learned how to learn, and those who have learned how to think.

Author Unknown

An immense amount of satisfaction and relief occurs when one completes educational goals. From *young* high school persons embarking on their new discoveries about themselves to seasoned adults who desire refinement or obtainment of skills to enhance their careers, education is rewarding. Obtaining a degree can be achieved online or in a traditional classroom. Options are available and with a few hours of research one can find the school, financial aid, and major before setting foot on a campus.

☼How The Information Was Found

Reading books helped to complete most of the research for this chapter, which was unlike the other chapters. The wealth of books listed in this section can be useful to students embarking on their higher education.

Web sites were most useful for disability research, and general financial aid information.

Colleges and Universities

Little or no difference exists between a college and a university. Within the US a school can name itself a college or university. One school might be a college, and another school might be a university, although they are of similar size and offer similar degrees and majors, as both colleges and universities are known to offer four-year degree as well as graduate degrees. The campus and class sizes vary depending on the institution.

Location	Sources
Web	www.allaboutcolleges.com www.collegeview.com www.Mapping-your-future.org www.gospelcom.net/cccu/ www.nccaa.org
Agencies	**Educational Resources Information Center (ERIC)** 2277 Research Blvd. MS4M Rockville, MD 20850 (800) LET-ERIC (800) 538-3742 **U.S. Department of Education** 400 Maryland Avenue, SW Washington, DC 20202-0498 (800) 872-5327

Private Colleges

Private colleges receive donations and tuition as their primary source of funding. The admissions criteria for private schools vary and are established by the institution. The criteria must meet state and federal guidelines, such as anti-discrimination and equal opportunity. The tuition for private schools also varies. Private schools often cost more than publicly funded institutions to offset the amount of money not received from government sources. The success of students at private schools is oftentimes greater because classrooms are smaller and students contribute more financially to encourage their involvement.

Public Colleges

Public colleges receive funding from tuition as well as state and federal governments. Because they receive money from the government, they must abide by all federal and state laws. Their sources for money are publicly disclosed as well as how the monies are used. The tuition is often less expensive than that for private colleges, therefore, they often enroll more students. The quality of education of a public school verses a private school is debatable. Some public colleges or universities have specialties that rival those at private schools.

Location	Source	
Web	www.mapping-your-future.org www.accesseric.org www.allaboutcolleges.com www.collegexpress.com www.ulinks.com www.collegeview.com www.collegenet.com	
Agencies	**Educational Resources Information Center (ERIC)** 2277 Research Blvd. MS4M Rockville, MD 20850 (800) LET-ERIC (800) 538-3742	**U.S. Department of Education** 400 Maryland Avenue, SW Washington, DC 20202-0498 (800) 872-5327

Community Colleges

Community colleges or junior colleges are increasing rapidly throughout the country. Public institutions strive to serve the academic needs of their community; they provide several academic options for those seeking a higher education as by offering associate degrees, certification in specialty areas, and extension courses; in addition, they provide intermediate college education for students who have not met the criteria for a university during their high school years; they operate similar to a university, in however they offer two-year credits; in almost all cases the credits can be applied to a four-year university. Students who cannot afford the high costs of a university can attend a community college for two years and transfer their credits to a university for the remaining two years of study (It is wise to consult with an adviser at the university you plan to attend for more information regarding which credits are transferable).

Location	Source
Books	Peterson's. *Peterson's Two Year Colleges, 2002.* Petersons Guides © 2001.
Web	www.ulinks.com www.mapping-your-future.org www.collegenew.com www.allaboutcollege.com www.aacc.nche.edu
Agency	**American Association of Community College** One Dupont Circle, NW. , Suite 410 Washington, DC 20036

ONLINE COLLEGES

One great benefit the Internet has provided is online education. For persons seeking a degree, this is an avenue worth investigating. Public as well as private colleges offer courses online. Amazingly one can receive a college degree via the Internet. What a great opportunity for those who have been denied an advance education in the past, an excellent vehicle for leveling the [academic] playing field.

Location	Source	
Books	Ice, Jerry, Paul Jay Edelson. *Complete Book of Distance Learning Schools: Everything You Need to Earn Your Degree Without Leaving Home.* Princeton Review Random House (c) 2001. Lorenzo, George. Teach Yourself e-college Today. Samms Publishing, © 2000. Petersons. Guide To Distance Learning Programs. Petersons © 2001.	Bear, John, Mariah Bear M.A., Tom C. Head. *Bears' Guide to Earning Degrees by Distance Learning* Ten Speed Press © 2001. Bear, John, Mariah Bear. *College Degrees by Mail & Internet: 100 Accredited Schools That Offer Bachelor's, Master's, Doctorates, and Law Degrees by Distance Learning.* Ten Speed Press © 2000
Web	www.collegeview.com www.allaboutcolleges.com www.collegeathome.com www.Petersons.com www.degree.net	

APPLYING FOR COLLEGE

College applications are long and intimidating. Finding the *right* answers to the questions causes many students stress: resources are available to help students and families with completing the application.

Location	Source	
Books	The College Board. *The College Board College Handbook 2003* College Entrance Examination Board © August 2002. Fiske, Edward B. *The Fiske Guide to Colleges 2003* Sourcebooks © 2002.	Rugg, Frederick E. *Rugg's Recommendations on the Colleges*, 19th Edition. Rugg's © 2002. Yale Daily News. *The Insider's Guide to the Colleges 2002* . Griffin Trade © 2001.
Web	http://collegeapps.about.com www.college-vists.com www.powerstudents.com www.collegeispossible.org	www.commonapp.org www.campustours.com www.studyabround.com
Agencies	**National Association for College Administration Counseling** 1631 Prince Street Alexandria, VA 22314-2818 (800) 822-6285	

PAYING FOR A HIGHER EDUCATION

Paying for the tuition costs accumulated over four years discourages some people from enrolling. With some clever planning you can attend college and receive a degree debt free. If you plan on attending a private "Ivy league school" then plan on paying around $25,000 per each year you attend, as opposed to public colleges, which tuition costs as low as $9,000 per year (and there are many that cost less). Even for the top schools there are methods of circumventing high costs by attending night college, receiving scholarships and grants, and/or learning online. With research the barrier to a higher education can easily be removed, as many options are available.

Many colleges and university care only that you can afford their tuition. If you have excellent grades, then you can receive scholarships to pay for the costs of your education. If you have wealthy parents, then they will pay. For information on paying for college see the next section.

Financial Aid for Colleges and Universities

Financial aid encompasses one or more sources for students to obtain funds for financing their education. Financial aid could include a package of loans, grants, work-study, and scholarships a student is likely to qualify for based on the grantors criteria. Financial aid offices located on college campuses can assist students with locating the right packages. A financial aid counselor /advisor is able to provide detailed information about the various options; he/she has knowledge hundreds of funding sources. Students, also, can locate their own resources. Several books specialize in listing financial aid resources for those of ethnic origins, gender, age, religious affiliation, and degree pursued to name a few. College aid sources for selected majors are also found at bookstores and in most college libraries. In addition to nationwide resources, schools offer scholarships and grants to qualifying students. Inquire about these resources from a financial aid advisor.

Location	Source
Books	Benjamin R. Kaplan *How to Go to College Almost for Free.* HarperCollins © 2001. The College Board College Entrance Examination Board. *The College Cost & Financial Aid Handbook 2003.* The College Board © 2002.
Web	www.studentloan.com www.tgslc.org www.access.group.org www.ed.gov/studentaid www.freschinfo.com www.nsf.gov www.estudentloan.com http://online.vophr.edc www.collegeview.com www.R1edu.org www.theoldschool.org www.hungerymind.com www.ed.gov www.savingforcollege.com
Agencies	**U.S. Department of Education** **Federal Student** P.O. Box 746000 **Aid** Atlanta, GA 30374 **Information** (800) 557-7394 **Center** (800) 4-Fed Aid P.O. Box 84 Washington, DC 20044 (800) 433-3243

Loans

Loans makeup the major source of financing for college students. Student loans are available through the state and federal governments and terms of repayment vary. For students who desire to complete a higher degree the loans can be deferred until education is completed.

Grants

Grants are distributed to students from either private or public agencies. Grants are monies given to the institutes for payment of students' tuition, which grants can cover all or part of the tuition. For more information on obtaining grants refer to the following resources:

Location	Source
Books	Petersons. *Scholarships, Grants & Prizes 2003* Petersons Guides © 2002. National Scholarship Research Service. *The Scholarship Book 2003: The Complete Guide to Private-Sector Scholarships, Fellowships, Grants and Loans for the Undergraduate.* Publisher: Prentice Hall Press © 2002.
Web	www.fafsa-ed.gov www.collegeview.com www.finaid.org www.ed.gov http://collegefund.org www.theoldschool.org http://easi.ed.gov/studentcenter www.nsf.gov www.salliemae.com www.finaid.org www.student.gov
Agencies	**Student Financial Assistance Program** **Federal Student Aid Information Center** **U.S. Department of Education** P.O. Box 84 400 Maryland Ave., SW Washington, DC Washington, DC 20202 20044 (202) 708-8242 (800) 433-3243

Fellowships

Fellowships are available to those who are completing a graduate degree. Similar to scholarships, fellowships are tailored to individuals who study a specific field. For example, there are fellowships for political science, biology, music, etc.

Location	Source	
Web	www.collegeview.com www.finaid.org	www.neh.gov www.students.gov
Agencies	**Fellowship and Stipends Division of Research and Education National Endowment for the Humanities** Room 318 Washington, DC 20506 (202) 606-8466	**International Education and Graduate Program Service** Office of Post Secondary Education Higher Education Programs U.S. Department of Education 1990 K Street, N.W. Washington, DC 20006-8521 (202) 502-7700

Scholarships

Similar to grants, scholarships are monies distributed by public or private agencies. Scholarships can be paid directly to a student to cover expenses for their education. The following resources are available to students and their families:

Location	Source	
Books	The College Board. *Scholarship Handbook 2003* (Scholarship Handbook, 2003). The College Entrance Examination Board © 2002.	Schlachter, Gail, R. David Weber. *Kaplan Scholarships 2003.* Kaplan © 2002.

Location	Source	
Web	www.scholarship-page.com www.fastweb.com www.fastap.org www.finaid.org www.theoldschool.org www.fregchinfo.com	www.collegeview.com www.scholarships.com www.srnexpress.com www.unct.org www.collegefunds.net www.freescholarships.com
Agencies	**United Negro College Fund** 8260 Willow Oaks Corporate Drive Fairfax, VA 22031 (703) 205-3400	**U.S. Department of Education** P.O. Box 74600 Atlanta, GA 30374 (800) 4-Fed Aid

TRADE SCHOOLS

Trade schools offer specialized education for certain occupations; they provide a focused academic program for career options that provide students with convenient hours to complete courses. Most people are familiar with truck driving schools and medical/dental assistant programs, which are examples of trade schools. Over the past 10 years, trade schools have grown to encompass reputable colleges like Devry® who offer degrees in specialized fields. Graduates learn the skills specifically used in their career because the education is exclusively focused on the major.

Locating a Trade School

When deciding on a trade school, do some research to ensure that the school is state licensed and does not have any complaints filed against them. Trade schools attract many interested students who are looking for an alternative to the high costs and long years of a traditional university education.

Location	Source	
Web	www.dlrn.org www.aips www.amionline.org http:// dentalglobe.com	www.wested.org www.uwex.com
Agencies	**American Institute for Paralegal Studies** 17 W 705 Butterfield Rd. Oakbrook Terrance, IL 60181 (800) 472-9404 **America's Second Harvest** 35 East Wacker Driver #2000 Chicago, IL 60601 (800) 771-2303	**Job Corps** 582 market St. Ste.719 San Francisco, CA 94104 16-24/ Years Old (877) 383-8731 (877) FUTURE-1 **U.S. Peace Corps** 11000 Wilshire Blvd. Suite 8104 Los Angeles, CA 90024 (800) 424-8580

Online Trade Schools / Distance Learning Courses

Similar to colleges and universities trade schools are now offering courses online. Schools specializing in certain studies such as paralegal studies, computer programming, accounting, health, nutrition and the list goes on are offering courses online. Some of the programs offer degrees as well as certifications.

Location	Source	
Books	Bear, John, Mariah Bear, Larry McQueary. *Bears' Guide to the Best Computer*	Lorenzo, George. *Teach Yourself e-college Today.* Samms © 2000.

Location	Source	
	Degrees by Distance Learning. Ten Speed Press © 2001.	Petersons. *Guide To Distance Learning Programs.* Petersons © 2001.
	Bear, John, Mariah Bear M.A., Mariah P. Bear, Tom C. Head. *Bears' Guide to Earning Degrees by Distance Learning.* Ten Speed Press © 2001.	
Web	www.wested.org www.uwex.com www.dlrn.org www.aips	www.amionline.org http://dentalglobe.com www.petersons.com

Financial Aid for Trade Schools

The costs for attending a trade college are less expensive than a traditional university, as they are typically located on smaller campuses, which reduce the overhead costs (for example, students do not pay for neon signs, the football team, and lawn maintenance) thus, the savings is passed onto the students.

GRADUATE SCHOOL

Graduate schools provide a specialized curriculum that combines true work experience with solid proven text methods. Persons with graduate degrees command high salaries because they are targeted for upper management positions. Receiving a post-graduate degree can be convenient. Large companies offer graduate courses onsite for employees and there are college campuses as well as online courses for persons interested in receiving an advance degree: there's even an online law school.

Location	Source	
Books	U.S. News & World Report U S News Specialty Marketing. *Best Graduate Schools 2003.* © 2002. Dave G., Mumby Ph.D. *Graduate School: Winning Strategies for Getting in With or Without Excellent Grades.* Proto Press © 1997.	Castellucci, Marion *Peterson's Game Plan for Getting into Graduate School* Petersons Guides © 2000.
Web	www.preyaw.com www.gradschool.com www.allaboutgradschool www.gradadvantage.org	www.ets.org www.mba.com www.gmac.com www.petersons.com
Agencies	**Graduate Management Admission Council** (703) 749-0131	

Online Graduate Schools

Those desiring to complete a higher education, online graduate schools are alternatives to traditional classroom settings. The schools are, typically, accredited and operated by major institutions.

Location	Source
Books	Petersons. *Guide To Distance Learning Programs.* Paperback p. 824,*2002ed.* © 2001. Bear, John, Mariah Bear M.A., Mariah P. Bear, Tom C. Head. *Bears' Guide to Earning Degrees by Distance Learning.* Ten Speed Press © 2001. Bear, John, Mariah Bear, Clinton Marsh. *Bears' Guide to the Best MBAs by Distance Learning.* Ten Speed Press © 2000. Bear, John , Mariah P. Bear. *College Degrees by Mail & Internet: 100 Accredited Schools That Offer Bachelor's, Master's, Doctorates, and Law Degrees by Distance Learning.* Ten Speed Press © 2001.
Web	www.mindedge.com www.petersons.com www.vmba.sbe.nova.edu

RESOURCES FOR DISABLED STUDENTS (PHYSICAL, LEARNING AND MENTAL DISABILITIES)

Students with disabilities are protected by federal (The Americans the with Disability Acts) and state laws to ensure that they receive, protection against discrimination, equal opportunities and, if need, supportive services. Schools have many services and aids available to those with disabilities including but not limited to counseling, advising, tutorials, academic support, referrals, classroom aides, readers, interpreters, note takers, special classes, special equipment, on-campus transportation, special parking, priority registration, test proctoring, specialized adaptive equipment, and high tech center with computer adaptations. An abundance of resources are available for those with disabilities, whether physical, learning or mental.

Location	Source	
	Strichart, Stephen S. (Ed.), Charles T., II Mangrum (Ed.). *Peterson's Colleges With Programs for Students With Learning Disabilities or Attention Deficit Disorders.* Peterson's Guides © 2000. Roslyn, Dolber. *College and Career Success for Students With Learning Disabilities.* McGraw-Hill/Contemporary Books © 1996.	Nadeau, Kathleen G. *Survival Guide for College Students With Add or Ld* Magination ©1994. Bramer, Jennifer S., Phd. *Succeeding in College With Attention Deficit Disorders: Issues and Strategies for Students, Counselors and Educators.* Specialty Press © 1996. Kravets, Marybeth, Imy F. Wax. *The K&W Guide to Colleges: For Students With Learning Disabilities or Attention Deficit Disorder.* Princeton Review © 2001.
Web	www.icweb.loc.gov/nls www.gsa.gov/frs www.ldanatl.org www.apa.org www.psych.org www.pueblo.gsa.gov	www.rfbd.org www.wrightslaw.com www.nami.org www.wrightslaw.com www.campusblues.com
Agencies	**National Library Services for the Blind and Physically Handicapped (NLS)**	**Recording for the Blind and Dyslexic** 20 Roszel Road Princeton, NJ 08540 (800) 221-4792

Location	Source
	C/O Library of Congress Washington, DC 20542 (800) 424-8567

National Cristina Foundation
500 West Putnam
Greenwich, CT 06830
(203) 863-9100

Federal Consumer Information Center Department
Dept. WWW
Pueblo, CO 81009

American Psychological Association (APA)
750 First Street, NE
Washington, DC 2002-4242
(800) 374-2721

Behavioral Health Services
15519 Crenshaw Blvd.
Gardena, CA. 90249
(310) 679-9126
(Disabled & Addicted)

American Psychiatric Association (APA)
1400 K Street, NW
Washington, DC 20005
(202) 682-6000

National Alliance for the Mentally Ill
Colonial Place Three
2107 Wilson Blvd.,
Suite 300
Arlington, VA 22201
(800) 950-NAMI (950-6264)
(703) 516-7227 (TTY)

PROBLEMS AT SCHOOL

For most students going to college is exciting and filled with hopes of achieving academic goals. Instances where students have difficulties with teachers and faculty exist. Ask a school advisor for a copy of the college's policy and procedures, particularly the campus policy for conflict resolution if the problem is not likely to be solved by communicating directly with the teacher or faculty member. The dean of student affairs may be able to provide a copy and assist with resolving the problem. In addition, school counselors can assist with resolving problems between students and faculty. Schools are taking great steps to assisting students as they are enrolled for academic purposes and not trouble.

Location	Source	
Web	www.youth.org www.outproud.org	www.teen-scene.org www.aclu.org
Agencies	**National Youth Advocacy Coalition** 16388 R Street, NW Suite 300 Washington, DC 20009 (800) 541-6922 **American Civil Liberties Union (ACLU)** 1400 20th St., NW, Suite 119 Washington, DC 20036 Tel.: (202) 457-0800 (Washington DC Office)	**U.S. Department of Education Office for Civil Rights** Customer Service Team Mary E. Switzer Bldg. 330 C St., SW Washington, DC 20202 (202) 205-5413

Discrimination

Persons who are the victim of discrimination based on your religion, race, gender, age (applies mainly to older adults), sexuality, or disability by a teacher or faculty member should notify their counselor, dean of student affairs, and the president of the college in writing. Contact an experienced attorney for assistance if the problem is not resolved or you are retaliated against as a result of voicing a complaint. Also, speak with other students who have had similar experiencing the problem may be commonly known among students.

Chapter 5

Employment, Unemployment and Self-Employment

In order that people may be happy in their work, these three things are needed: They must be fit for it; they must not do too much of it; and they must have a sense of success in it.

John Ruskin

 hether beginning a first job, moving onto new opportunities, or deciding to take the leap and venture out to wage independence this chapter is for you.

☼How The Information Was Found

Excellent books by employment experts and lawyers have been written to help persons become aware of their rights in the work place. Several of those books are referenced throughout this section. Researching specialty bookstores, asking human resource persons, and visiting college bookstores, especially those offering advance degrees, helped with locating books contained in this chapter.

The web sites were located by performing searches and by following links from major web sites. Agencies referenced in this chapter were located when interviewing persons in the labor field, in books, and through government directories.

EMPLOYMENT

Most persons need to find some form of income to cover their costs for living. For persons who do not have any experience with locating employment this process initially can be intimidating, even for entry-level positions. The resources provided throughout this chapter are designed to make employment searching and career decisions easier.

EMPLOYMENT INTERVIEWS

Attire for an interview should be conservative and professional, wear neatly pressed clothing and clean shoes. The interviewer shouldn't focus on your wrinkled shirt more than what you're saying. Finding work isn't as difficult as getting work. The interview is just as important as your resume; it is during this time when the interviewer matches the information on the resume to the personality before him/her. I have conducted several interviews and I'm often amazed at how the personality of the candidate does not match the resume before me.

Be as confident and secure about yourself and skills as written on paper. An interview is your first opportunity to impress. Nothing goes perfectly, don't focus on perfection as much as personality – be yourself.

A few rules are recommended when applying for work:

- Schedule interviews, which require a commute, during non rush hour times, to ensure that you are composed prior to the interview.
- Read about a company online, you will appear knowledgeable and interested in the company's products or services.

- Prepare a resume, although this is not necessary for all types of jobs.
- Dress professionally. Wear the best articles of clothing and ensure that it is pressed to give a clean and neat looking appearance. Do not use perfume or cologne many people have allergies and certain scents aggravate their condition.
- Be aware of personal hygiene. Take along mints in the event of a long wait before being interviewed.
- Shake hands with the interviewer and those whom introduce themselves.
- Practice answering questions with a friend. Take deep breaths and carefully think about the question before responding.
- Relax - Relax - Relax! Do not be intimidated by the interviewer, often times they are nervous too. Remember that they are looking for someone who quickly ascertains information, a self-starter who is eager to work and does not require lots of direction. The company wants someone in control of their emotions so RELAX!

FINDING EMPLOYMENT

The number one rule for job seekers is to not spend long hours looking for a job. Sending out hundreds of resumes and receiving hundreds of rejection letters inevitably destroys your confidence. Take time to focus on what you truly want.

With the advent of the Internet searching for employment is convenient. For those who purchase classified papers, searching for hours now takes seconds online. However, the best resource for jobseekers remain friends who

Job Opportunity for The Blind
National Federation of
The Blind
1800 Johnson St.
Baltimore, MD 21230
(410) 659-9314

provide valuable job leads. With both options deployed your next job is near.

Books are available on locating jobs within the government, in social work, legal and other industry specific fields. Start with what you enjoy doing and what talents are natural to you. Self-assessment books help to find hidden talents. Persons who excel at everything they do, the key to success is selecting one skill to pursue. As you continue to succeed, explore other talents. You may find that your employer is supportive of their employees who take on additional tasks, especially if it does not involve additional pay.

Personality Assessments

High schools and colleges have questionnaires available to students who need help determining their career path; these questions are typically called career assessments. The questions trace consistency with answers in order to arrive at what, skills are natural to the participant. For example, a question may ask if you enjoy the outdoors, and if it is consistently answered throughout the assessment it may suggest that person should consider occupations that involve being outside. Answer the questions honestly; do not try to fudge the results. The goal is to see what the paper thinks you should do, not what you will do. The results are not *set in stone*; if you disagree with the outcome, give it some thought. Ask family and friends about the results and carefully evaluate their opinion.

Location	Source
Book	Tieger, Paul D., Barbara Barron-Tieger. Do What You Are. Little, Brown, & Co. © 2001.
Web	www.careerplanit.com www.careerpathsonline.com

Location	Source
	www.careers.com
	www.advisorteam.com
	www.quintcareers.com
	http://self-directed-search.com

Job Placement for students

Colleges have job placement offices where enrolled students can search for employment. Hiring companies are oftentimes located in the local community, which makes commuting to work and school convenient for employed students. In addition, most colleges hire students to work on campus. Finding the *high* paying on campus jobs is more challenging and may require networking with the facility to obtain.

The web site www.jobtrack.com allows students at colleges across the country to search for jobs posted on their employment boards. Schools may have a code for students to enter; the code is easily obtained from the job placement counselor at the college. Not only does the site provide referrals to local jobs, but co·ops and internships as well.

Location	Source	
Web	www.jobtrack.com www.adguide.com www.mapping-your-furture.org www.black-collegian.com www.studentadvantage.com www.internshipprograms.com	www.careermosaic.com www.collegegrad.com www.epinions.com www.adguide.com www.jobs.com www.4work.com
Agencies	**Division of Policy Developments Student financial**	**Federal Student Aid Information Center** P.O. Box 84

Location	Source	
	Assistance Programs	Washington, DC 20044
	Office of Assistant	(800) 433-3243
	Secretary for Post	
	Secondary Education	
	400 Maryland Ave., SW	
	Washington, DC 20202	
	(202) 708-8242	

Employment Agencies

Employment agencies serve a dual need; they match candidates (those seeking employment) with hiring companies and find qualified candidates for companies to choose. Temp agencies only place *temporary* workers: those looking for work on short-term bases. If the company desires to retain the person, then an agreement is made between the employment agency and company for the person to be hired full-time. Agencies often have a specialized field in which they place candidates such as accounting, general office, engineering, software programmers, etc. In past years agencies have merged to form larger employment companies that outsource work to their sister companies to whom they're affiliated.

Every hour an employee works the agency receives a percentage of the billable pay. For example, if an agency places a worker at $25.00 per hour the agency receives $15.00 so that total amount of money billed to the company is $40.00 per hour. So why do companies pay employment agencies? If they have knowledgeable recruiters on staff, then they are able to quickly locate people with skills that are in demand. The agency checks school and work references, which takes these tasks away from companies who have a desire to fill a position immediately. Companies often use agencies in addition to performing their own search, so it is a wise for workers to seek employment on their own as well as using an agency.

Agencies must comply with state and federal laws that include no discrimination, offer health benefits (for states that require companies with 50 or more employees), and unemployment when a workers job is completed, to name a few examples.

Location	Source	
Books	*The Directory of Executive Recruiters 2002.* Kennedy Information © 2001. Hunter, Darrell W. Gurney. *Headhunters Revealed! Career Secrets for Choosing and Using Professional Recruiters.* Arts Publishing © 2000. Schoyen, Christian, Nils Rasmussen *Secrets of the Executive Search Experts.* AMACOM © 1999.	Smooch S. Reynolds John Wiley & Sons. *Be Hunted! 12 Secrets to Getting on the Headhunter's Radar Screen* © 2001.
Web	www.dice.com www.headhunter.net	www.monster.com http://careers.yahoo.com

Newspapers

Classified ads placed in newspapers is another good method for locating employment. Companies who search for employees will often place ads in the newspapers. Most companies are reluctant to place classified as ads they received a host of applicants whose experiences may or may not match their criteria. For those whose background matches the company's expectations, as they have weeded through many resumes to find you, which is encouraging. Companies oftentimes are willing to invest the time to locate the *right* person for the job.

Location	Source
Web	www.latimes.com
	www.careerpath.com
	www.nytimes.com
	www.washingtonpost.com
	www.bostonglobe.com

Career Fairs

Companies and agencies searching for desired candidates participate in job fairs. Businesses are able to get a first-hand feel of candidates to fill open positions. Some high schools and colleges host career fairs for students desiring work, especially those who are graduating soon. Representatives from several companies and agencies present options to candidates desiring work at their location. Typically there is no fee for attending candidates; the company pays for booths and materials. Job and career fairs are advertised through local media source; such as radios, newspapers and massive marketing on college campuses. For those interested in job fairs see www.joboptions.com.

The Internet

One of the best uses for the Internet is locating employment. Resources for job seekers are available for locating the right job or career, from general labor to top executives finding a job has been made easy online. Books have been written that categorize careers and combines resources where one can begin looking, for those who find the online sources too expansive. Companies may choose to post career or job openings directly on their site – persons desiring to work at specific company can surf their web site for openings.

Location	Source
Books	Baker, Wayne E. *Networking Smart: How to build Relationship for Personal and Organizational Success.* McGraw-Hill, © 1994. Marler, Patty and Jan Mattia Bailey. *Networking Made Easy.* VGM Career Horizons, © 1997. Tullier, Michelle L. *Networking for Everyone: Connecting with People for Career and Job Success.* Jist works, © 1998. Kramer, Marc. *Power Networking: Using the Contracts You Don't Even Know You Have to Succeed in the Job You Want.* VGM Career Horizons, © 1997. Dikel, Riley Margaret, Frances E. Roehm. *The Guide To Internet Job Searching 2000-01ed.* VGM Career Horizons, © 2000.
Web	www.jobbankusa.com www.monster.com www.careerbuilder.com www.dice.com www.hotjobs.com www.ajb.com www.headhunter.net www.workers.gov

TYPES OF WORKERS

Companies classify workers according to their work status.
Four commonly referred to types of workers exist:

Full-time

Full-time is a replacement of the term *permanent,*
which applies to persons who work 40 or more hours
per week. To avoid legal liabilities companies have
abandoned the word *permanent* when referring to an
employee's work status. Full-time employees are
either exempt (a salaried employee who is not paid
overtime) or nonexempt (paid overtime).

Part time Employee

Part-time employees work a reduced hour schedule.
Depending on the organization and [4]state laws, these
employees may receive employer paid benefits. Part-
time employment is ideal for those with children as it
affords time away from home to earn an income yet it
allows for time to care for children. The health care
industry hires a large amount of part-time workers.
Companies who staff personnel for general office
duties and mail room clerks also find needs for part-
time workers to fill those positions. Often times those
who are returning from a medical leave afforded time
to work part-time while recovering. Students,
particularly college students, can contact the job
placement department for referrals to part-time
employers.

---

[4]To locate information regarding your state laws for employment
benefits contact the Equal Employment Opportunity Commission
by using their web site or refer to the Appendix A.

If you are currently employed as a full-time employee and desire to work part-time, ask your employer if you can switch your hours to part-time, or if there are other positions at the company which can use a part-time employee. Some employers allow their employees to work part-time at home and part-time in the office. Most people accomplish more work at home, as they do not want to appear as if they're slackers, but I would caution that children and family could interfere with work time at home.

Temporary

There is still no thrill quite like doing something you didn't know you could do.
-Marjorie Holmes

Temp workers are hired for a specified period of time. An increasing number of employers hire temporary employees for an average of three-months, although the times vary according to the assignment. At the end of the three-month period, agencies can transfer the employee's status to full-time, extend the labor contract with the company or terminate the working relationship, depending on the workers performance. Prospective employees can seek employment directly with a company for temporary work and negotiate the terms as opposed to using a third party agency: which saves the company placement fees and provides immediate employment to the individual. However, employers like to have temporary employees pre-screened, which could involve typing, data entry, software, accounting, and drug tests. Prospective employees with strong references often overcome the desire for the skill tests. A company doctor, personal family doctor or a local clinic can perform a drug test at a minimum charge, usually for $10-15.

Temporary Jobs
www.Net-Temps.com

Contractor/Consultants

Something made greater by ourselves and in turn that makes us greater.

Maya Angelou

Contractors are self-employed individuals who pay taxes separate from the employing company. Prior to commencing work both, the contractor and company, sign a contract agreeing on the terms of work. The contract is legally binding and should always be in writing. The contract should explicitly state what the contractor is being hired to complete. A new agreement should be drawn when the scope of the contract changes. Contractors are not required to follow rules of the organization as they are not employees, but often they are asked to obey company standards and they do so at their own discretion.

Contractors bill the company directly for services and are considered a creditor to the organization; they are often required to submit a time card to the payroll department for hours worked. The benefit of contract employment is that it provides a higher pay than regular employment, as the employment does not pay benefits. The employer pays the contractor for hours worked only, they do not pay medical, dental, vacation or sick time.

Location	Source
	Roberts, Lisa M. *How to Raise a Family and A Career Under One Roof.* New Beginnings, © 1998.
Books	Folger, Liz. *The Stay-At-Home Mom's Guide to Making Money.* New Beginnings, © 1998.
	Moore, Jimmy. *Advancing into Temp, Contract, and Consulting Jobs.* iUniverse © 2001.

Location	Source	
Web	www.sologig.com	www.gohome.com
	www.workfromhome.com	www.allfreelance.com
	www.advancing.ws	

MINORS IN THE WORK PLACE

The age for minors workers vary, but most states allow children to work under special provision such as a workers permit, which can be obtained from a school counselor or work program administrator (a workers permit allows minors to work for a specified period of time). The permit must be signed by a parent or guardian and must include the location of the prospective employer. In addition, the work schedule must not conflict with school hours.

For more information contact your states Equal Opportunity Development Department (see Appendix A).

Location	Source
Web	www.furture.scan.com
	www.gettingreal.com
	www.abanet.org

MINORITIES IN THE WORK PLACE

Workers of varying ethnic backgrounds have made huge advancements in the workplace. Executives, judges, doctors, and other minority professionals are found at the head of renowned institutions. Some have chosen to operate their own successful companies that provide opportunities to those who have traditionally been passed over. With all of these successes there remains those who are shut, kicked, and knocked out the workforce for no reason other than their race. Employed workers also face constant stereotyping and insults in order to earn a living. Members of the same ethnic group chair numerous professional organizations, which can prove supportive in succeeding in your profession.

Location	Source	
Book	Bernbach, Jeffrey M. *Job Discrimination II: How to Fight, How to Win.* Voir Dire Press ©1998.	
Web	www.nativeweb.org www.netnoir.com www.gaywork.com www.saludos.com www.diversityemployment.com www.minorities-jb.com www.diversitycareers.com	www.equalrights.org www.blackwork.com www.hisp.com www.saludos.com www.naacp.org www.abanet.org
Agencies	**Equal Employment Opportunity Commission** (800) 699-EEOC **Equal Rights Advocates** (415) 621-0672 (800) 839-4372 (415) 621-0505	**U. S. Commission on Civil Rights** 624 9th St., NW Washington, DC 20425 (800) 552-6843 **National Job Problem Hotline** (800) 522-0925

Typically the person to whom you report to should be notified if discrimination occurres, as long as he/she is not involved in the alleged acts, and a human resources department executive. According to the law you cannot be fired or punished for notifying your employer of discriminatory acts this is termed retaliation. Consult the EEOC, (see *Appendix A*) and a knowledgeable and experienced labor law attorney for assistance.

SENIORS IN THE WORK PLACE

The Age Discrimination in Employment Act (ADEA) prohibits employers from discrimination against employees between the ages of 40 and 70 (however it does not apply to jobs where age is a *bona fide occupational qualification*, BFOQ, reasonably necessary to the essence of the business). The ADEA governs all public and private (private companies with 20 or more employees) employers, including union members. States have enacted more stringent laws that offer additional protection to older employees. The state laws can prove to be a first course of action to seeking remedies, as many state laws are tougher than federal laws and provide greater monetary damage awards. The ADEA combined with the Americans with Disabilities Act (ADA), and Older Workers Benefit Protection Act ([5]OWBPA) provides a system for protecting for aging Americans.

Location	Source	
Web	www.seniorjobbank.com www.equalrights.org	www.dol.gov www.abanet.org
Agencies	**Department of Labor** **Office of Public Affairs** Room S1032 200 Constitution Ave. NW Washington, DC 20210 (202) 693-4650	**Senior Job Bank** P.O. Box 30064 Savannah, GA 31410

The following are examples of age discriminatory conduct:

---

[5] An amendment to the ADEA that established employee benefits amounts, conditions, compensation and privileges of employment. It also requires employers either to provide older works with benefits equal to those of younger workers or to incur the same cost for providing a benefit for an older worker as for a younger worker.

~ Force older workers into early retirement.

~ Refuse of hire older workers.

~ Terminated and a younger person is hired for the same position.

~ Retaliated against for opposing employment practices that discriminate based on age or for filing an age discrimination charge.

~ Offered a wavier (severance package) in addition to an incentive to retire or when being fired.

WOMEN IN THE WORK PLACE

Within the last few decades, women have made significant career advancements such as owning and managing successful small and large companies. Unfortunately, it is not uncommon for women to face discrimination or run into the proverbial *glass ceiling*. Women have taken charge by enforcing their legal rights and forming organizations that support their advancement.

Location	Source	
Books	Sack, Stephen Mitchell *The Working Woman's Legal Survival Guide*, Prentice Hall Press, © 1998. Prayor, Gale. *Nursing Mother, Working Mother.* New Beginnings, © 1998. Jones, Nancy L. Esq. with Phil Philcox. *The Woman's Guide to Legal Issues.* Renaissance Books, © 2000.	
Web	www.advancingwoman.com www.witi.com www.womanconnect.com www.womenemployed.org www.feminist.com/fairpay www.nationalpartnership.org www.equalrights.org	www.whrnet.org www.Nate.com www.bwni.com www.bizwomen.com www.aflcio.org www.woman.com www.wowonline.org
	Business Women Network	**National**

Location	Source	
Agencies	1990 M Street, NW Washington, DC 20036 (800) 48-WOMEN	**Partnership for** **Women & Families** 1875 Connecticut Avenue, NW, Suite 650
	Wider Opportunities for **Women** 1001 Connecticut Avenue, NW Suite 930 Washington, DC 20036 (202) 464-1596	Washington, DC 20009 Phone: 202-986- 2600
	9 to 5 National **Association of Working** **Women** (800) 522-0925	**National** **Association for** **Female Executives** P.O. Box 469031 Escondido, CA 92046-9925
	Equal Rights Advocates (415) 621-0672 (800) 839-4372 (415) 621-0505	(800) 634-NAFE **Equal Employment** **Opportunity** **Commission** (800) 699-EEOC

RIGHTS OF EMPLOYEES

All employees should be aware of their rights in the workplace. Knowing your rights before a problem arise can circumvent many issues that can escalate to termination or civil suit. Most companies have policies and procedures that document the employer's responsibility well as expectations. Some are detailed so that employees are aware of what to do when a problem occurs. Employees should read the policies and procedures carefully to gain a general understanding of the companies position on correcting and resolving issues. In addition, read the information from the following source to gain more insight into legal rights of workers.

Location	Source	
Book	The American Bar Association. *Guide to Workplace Law.* Three Rivers Press, © 1997. Joel, Lewin G., III. *Every Employee's Guide to the Law: Everything You Need to Know About Your Rights in the Workplace and What to Do If They Are Violated.* Pantheon Books ©1997. Fick, Barbara J. *The American Bar Association Guide to Workplace Law: Everything You Need to Know About Your Rights As an Employee or Employer.* Times Books © 1997. Outten, Wayne N. *The Rights of Employees and Union Members: The Basic ACLU Guide to the Rights of Employees and Union Members,* Southern Illinois Univ © 1994.	
Web	www.equalrights.org www.dol.gov www.eeoc.gov www.4women.gov	
Agencies	**Equal Employment Opportunity Commission** (800) 669-EEOC **Equal Rights Advocate** (415) 621-0672 (800) 839-4372 (415) 621-0505	**National Job Problem Hotline** (800) 522-0925 **National Victims Center** (703) 276-2880 (800) FYI-CALL **Women's Bureau** (800) 827-5335

Rights of Pregnant Women

Most employers are supportive of women employees who choose to raise a family and continue with their career. Some employers have onsite day care centers or pay a portion of their employees day care expenses. Expecting women should continue to be treated fairly and equally as other employees, unless there is a Bona Fide Occupational Qualification (BFOQ) for not being pregnant (*for more information see Seniors In The Workplace in this chapter*).

Sexual Harassment

With the many laws that protect workers and the damages that can be obtained, it is baffling that persons continue to regard others as sexual objects. Disturbed individuals that see others as objects to fulfill their twisted fantasies and not as true professionals should not be tolerated. See an attorney who specializes in seeking remedies for workers who have been subjected to this behavior. Before contacting an attorney become familiar with the employment/labor laws, as persons who believe that they have been sexually harassed must notify management, before making a claim. Although the book resources listed below are specific to women, sexually harassed men can use the information.

Location	Source
Books	Sack, Stephen Mitchell *The Working Woman's Legal Survival Guide*, Prentice Hall Press, © 1998. Jones, Nancy L. Esq. with Phil Philcox. *The Woman's Guide to Legal Issues.* Renaissance Books, © 2000.
Web	www.dol.gov/dol/wb/ www.eeoc.gov
	U.S. Department of **Equal Rights**

Location	Source	
Agencies	**Labor Women's Bureau** 200 Constitution Avenue, NW Room S-3311 Washington, DC 20210 (202) 219-6652 (800) 326-2577 (TDD) **Equal Employment Opportunity Commission** 1400 L St., NW Washington, DC 20005 (800) 669-4000	**Advocate** 1663 Mission St. #550 San Francisco, CA 94103 (800) 839-4372 **National Victim's Center** (703) 276-2880 (800) FYI-CALL

Rights of the Disabled

Employers have a responsibility not to discriminate against persons who apply for positions and need special accommodations; it is after applying for employment that disabled persons face the greatest infringement of their rights.

Location	Source	
Web	www.dav.org www.disabilityresources.org www.jobaccess.org www.bazelon.org www.lookingglass.org	
Agencies	**Disabled American Veterans**	**Job Accommodation Network**

Location	Source	
	3725 Alexandria Pike Cold Spring, KY 41076 Phone: (859)441-7300 **Handicapped Law** **Compliance** 1265 Kendell Dr., Suite 5211 San Bernardino, CA 92407 (909) 883-9927 **American Civil Liberties** **(ACLU)** **American Civil Liberties** **Union (ACLU)** 1400 20th St., NW, Suite 119 Washington, DC 20036 Tel.: (202) 457-0800 (Washington DC Office)	(800) 232- 9675(voice/TDD) (800) 526- 7234(Voice/TDD) (800) 526- 2262(Canada) **Association For** **Retarded Citizens** 2456 Jacksboro Hwy. Forth worth, TX 76114 (817) 624-7001 **U. S. Commission On** **Civil Rights** 624 9th St., NW Washington, DC 20425 (800) 552-6843

Drug Screening

Companies drug screening applicants prior to employment and perform random drug screening has become popular. The drug screens are voluntarily and employers cannot force employees perform these tests, although they can make it a condition for employment. Employers often *ask* potential employee candidates to sign a wavier or agreement to the terms of employment before drug screening. Persons who take medications that contain drugs should bring a list to the lab where the drug test is performed; the prescription will coincide with the lab results. Inform the company that you take certain medications that contain drugs prior to taking the test. State laws vary as to the legal rights employees have for refusing drug screening. Consult with an experienced labor/employment attorney for more information.

Workers Compensation

Workers compensation is an insurance that is paid by the employer in the event an employee suffers an injury on the job (it also can apply to employees who suffer injuries while traveling to or because of their work). The payout varies depending on the state where the company is located. Persons who are injured receive a percentage of their weekly pay up to the maximum payout amount.

In addition to pay employees receive training, if necessary, and medical benefits. In place of litigation employees and employers arbitrate their differences until an agreement is reached. For information on your states workers compensation laws contact a knowledgeable attorney.

Location	Source	
	Hood, Jack B., Benjamin A Hardy Jr., Harold S. Lewis Jr. *Workers Compensation and Employee Protection Laws*. West Group ©1999.	Ball, Christopher A. *Take Charge of Your Workers' Compensation Claim: An A to Z Guide for Injured Employees*
Book	Hood, Jack B., Benjamin A., Jr Hardy, Harold S., Jr Lewis *Workers' Compensation and Employee Protection Laws* West Wadsworth © 1999.	Nolo Press© 2002. (contact publisher for book status)

UNEMPLOYMENT

Finding oneself unemployed whether voluntarily or against your will can be the beginning of a positive life change. Persons can take time to develop businesses or locate another position that suits their skills and desires. Unemployment can provide time required to evaluate the course of your future and help to make clear your new direction.

For an entire day do not think about obtaining a new position. Don't think or talk about the people you just left at the *old* company. Find a spot that you enjoy and relax. During the time of relaxing the mind is able to be creative and seek out new and better opportunities.

Always talk with some who's ready to listen; this sounds lame, but hearing yourself talk about the issue(s) that are upsetting does help. The answer lies within you and talking your way through a potential problem often reassures one of their abilities.

Location	Source	
Books	Melancon, Robert M. *The Secrets of Executive Search ... Professional Strategies for Managing Your Personal Job Search.* Melancon & Company © 2000.	Sklover, Alan L. *Fired, Down-Sized, or Laid-Off: What Your Employer Doesn't Want You to Know About How to Fight Back.* Henry Holt © 2000.
	Sack, Steven Mitchell. *Getting Fired: What to Do If You're Fired, Downsized, Laid Off, Restructured,*	Tobias, Paul H., Susan Sauter, *Job Rights & Survival Strategies: A Handbook for Terminated Employees*

Location	Source
	Discharged, Terminated, or Forced to Resign. Warner Books © 2000. — National Employee Rights Institute © 1997.
Web	www.fuckedcompany.com www.lectlaw.com/files/emp43.htm www.quintcareers.com/getting_fired.html www.severancefaq.com

WRITING A RESUME

Writing a resume isn't difficult as the prospective employer does most of the work in advance. Matching your experience to their needs is simple by incorporating their requirements. List the companies that you have worked for and underneath a brief, one sentence, description of your duties combined with your accomplishments.

For those who have had problems with previous employers consider not listing them on your resume even though it is against the law for companies to make derogatory statements about their current and previous employees. If you had problems with one person, then give the name of another manager or co-worker who can provide positive insight into your work.

- The first step in creating a resume is selecting a style. Select a format that can expand as the examples of work completed grows.
- Always remember to put your best foot forward. Adding an *objective* section, which briefly explains career objectives, is a personal decision. Omit the objective to

allow for room on two pages if you an expansive three page resume. People with two or more careers; writing two separate resumes is best instead of combining all the information into one resume. When a position that fits either of your careers arise, simply send the appropriate resume.

- Some people have many degrees and several accomplishments during educational years. While others have spent many years working and gaining real-life experience. The applicable choice should be the second item.
- Experience can be bulleted items highlighting the responsibilities with previous employers and your accomplishments.

  - **Duties without accomplishment.**

    Responsible for transporting nitrogen gas from coast to cost.

  - **Sample of duty along with accomplishment:**

    Transported nitrogen gas from east to west costs without incident, and consistently met scheduled deadlines.

- The resume finale is additional accomplishments and/or skills. Include additional accomplishments that will be of value to a perspective employer. If the position is for a nuclear scientist then chances are it doesn't matter that you type 75 words per minute. What employers may find important are the papers you've written, committee membership, symposiums attended, etc. in addition to education and experiences. For technically savvy persons listing technical capabilities is important.

A resume is a written brochure about oneself. Remember to use plenty of positive adjectives when describing accomplishments and experiences.

Location	Source	
Books	Kennedy, Joyce Lain. *Resumes For Dummies* 3rd ed. IDG Books, © 2000. Parker, Yana. *Dam Good Resumes*. Ten Speed Press, © 1996.	Asher, Donald. *Asher's Bible of Executive Resumes and How to Write Them*. Ten Speed Press © 1996.
Web	www.jobweb.com/Resumes_Interviews/default.htm www.certifiedresumewriters.com	
Agency	**Professional Association of Résumé Writers & Career Coaches** 1388 Brightwaters Blvd., N.E. St. Petersburg, FL 33704 (727) 821-2274 (800) 822-7279	

STARTING A BUSINESS

Owning and operating a business is not solely for those who have lots of wealth or degrees, it's for anyone who aspires to profit from their experiences.

Location	Source	
Books	Daily, Frederick W. *Tax Saving for Small Business*. Nolo Press, © 2001.	Carter, Gary W. *Taxes Made Easy for Your Home-Based Business*. John Wiley & Sons, ©

Location	Source	
		2000.
	Frederick, Dailey W. *J.K Lesser's Tax Savvy For Small Business.* Nolo Press, © 2001.	Fishman, Stephen. *Working For Yourself.* Nolo Press, © 2001.
	Pakroo, Peri H. *The Small Business Start-up Kit.*	Kamoroff, Bernard B. *422 Tax Deduction for Business & Self-Employed Individuals.* Bell Springs Publishing, © 2001.
	Green, Charles H. *The SBA Loan Book.* Adams Media Corporation, © 1999.	
	Lewin, Elizabeth S. *Kiss the Rat Race Good-Bye.* Walker & Company, © 1994.	
Web	www.mycounsel.com www.nolo.com www.gohome.com www.workfromhome.com www.cfda.gov www.Youachieve.com	
Agencies	**Small Business Administration** (800) 827-5722	

Sole Proprietorship

A sole proprietorship is a business whose one/sole owner makes all business decisions and assumes all business liabilities. This is the least complex form of business ownership. Sole Proprietor's can apply for a federal employer identification number through the IRS as an alternative to using your social security number. To ensure the business does not cease in case of the death of the owner it's important to state who the business should be transferred to in the event of death.

Partnership

A partnership is a business owned by two or more people. Some states require written agreements between partners – it's wise to have a written agreement. Each partner is responsible for the liabilities and debts incurred by the business. As with Sole Proprietorships, a partnership is easy to begin.

Corporation

A corporation is a type of business structure created and regulated by state law. What sets the corporation apart from all other types of businesses is that a corporation is an independent legal entity, separate from the people who own, control and manage it. In other words, corporation and tax laws view the corporation as a legal "person," meaning that the corporation can enter into contracts, incur debts and pay taxes like most individuals. Another important characteristics that result from the corporation's separate existence: a corporation does not dissolve when its owners (shareholders) change or die, and the owners of a corporation are not personally responsible for the corporation's debts; this is called limited liability. Many different types of corporations exist: non-profit, S, C, LLP.

C-Corporation

The label, "C-Corporation" merely refers to a regular, state- formed corporation. To be formed, an Incorporator must file Articles of Incorporation and pay the requisite state fees and prepaid taxes with the appropriate state agency (usually, the Secretary of State).

Limited Liability Company (LLC)

A limited liability company (LLC), on the other hand, does offer limited personal liability, like a corporation. And while formal paperwork is required to form an LLC -- also like a corporation -- running an LLC is less complicated. LLC owners do not have to hold regular ownership and management meetings or follow other corporate formalities. In contrast, partnerships, sole proprietorships and LLCs are not taxed on business profits; instead, the profits "pass through" the business to the owners, who report business income or losses on their personal tax returns.

Nonprofit Corporation

A nonprofit corporation is a corporation formed to carry out a charitable, educational, religious, literary or scientific purpose. A nonprofit can raise much-needed funds by receiving public and private grant money and donations from individuals and companies. The federal and state governments do not generally tax nonprofit corporations on money they make that is related to their nonprofit purpose, because of the benefits they contribute to society.

Buying a Franchise

Franchise ownership can be a secure investment for persons who desire to own a business whose brand name has had proven success. Franchise owners do not need to pour money into advertising, as the business has an established name and reputation. Different types of franchises are available; such as automotive services, employment agencies, dry cleaning and restaurants to name a few examples.

Location	Source	
Books	Rule, Roger C. *No Money Down: Financing for Franchising* PSI Research - Oasis Press © 1998.	Tomzack, Mary E. *Tips & Traps When Buying a Franchise* Source Book Pubns © 1999.
	Shivell, Kirk. *The Franchise Kit/a Nuts-And-Bolts Guide to Owning and Running a Franchise Business* McGraw-Hill Trade © 1995.	
Web	www.franchising.org www.franchisesolutions.com www.franchisedoc.com www.franchise.com www.aafd.org	
Agencies	**American Association of Franchisees and Dealers** PO Box 81887 San Diego, CA 92138-1887 (800) 733-9858 **American Franchisee Association** 53 West Jackson Boulevard, Suite 205 Chicago, Illinois 60604 Telephone: 312-431-0545	

Chapter 6

Doctors, Dentists, and Ophthalmologist

> *... in order to be a good doctor a man must*
> *also have a good character, that is to say,*
> *whatever weaknesses and foibles he may*
> *have, he must love his fellow human beings in*
> *the concrete and desire their good before his*
> *own.*
>
> W. H. Auden

The greatest relief during a health crisis is knowing that your life is in knowledgeable hands. For anyone who has undergone a health emergency the fear that your life can end in a matter of breaths lingers long after the crisis is resolved · for many people it reshapes their life forever.

☼How The Information Was Found

Locating resources about health care professionals is made convenient by using the Internet. Many of the resources referred in this chapter were located via the World Wide Web, including the books and agency references.

As you research the topics ensure that your first stop is the Internet as the websites listed provide and/or direct visitors to useful information about health care.

TYPES OF MEDICAL INSURANCE

With the many health care coverage plans (HMOs, PPOs, POSs) most of us need H·E·L·P to understand what each one does, why they do it, and how much it costs. The following sections discuss the different plans and addresses major advantages. The pricing for each plan is obtained from your human resources representative, union representative, medical insurance broker or by contacting the insurance provider directly. Some topics have combined resources located at the end of their topics.

Health Maintenance Organization (HMO)

HMO is widely known and used by millions of people because the plans offer fixed payments over a period. An HMO is a single organization that is either contracted or sponsored by the government, schools, unions, employers, insurance companies and hospital/medical plans. For *group* models physicians are employed directly with the HMO. Participants receive enrollment through an employer or union who pays partial, if not all, enrollment fees or by purchasing an individual plan. The participants have no out of pocket costs to pay (except for minimal co·payments if applicable) to the medical practitioner even for individual plans. Lately there has been bad publicity in the news regarding HMO's for rejecting and delaying decisions for persons who have dire needs. Resources have been added for additional information for HMO participants who have received rejection for vital medical services.

Location	Source	
	www.ncqa.org	www.hcfa.gov
Web	www.jcaho.org	www.iii.org

Location	Source	
Agencies	**Office of Prepaid Health Care Operation and Oversite** Office of Operation Health Care Financing Administration 7500 Security Blvd. Baltimore, MD 21244 (410) 786-3000 **Joint Commission on Accreditation of Health Care Organizations** (800) 994-6610	**National Committee for Quality Assurance (NCQA)** (888) 275-7585 Verify if HMO plan is accredited and their quality rating. **Agency For Healthcare Research and Quality (AHRQ)** Publications Clearing House P.O. Box 8547 Silver Springs, MD 20907-8547 (800) 358-9298

Point of Service Plans (POS) & Preferred Provider Organization (PPO)

Health care organizations or other third party insurers contract doctors to provide services at a discounted rate. The discounted rate is passed onto the customer in exchange for prompt payment of services and an agreement to visit only the doctors associated with the plan (unless combined with a POS, see the following paragraph). PPOs offer flexibility to patients in exchange for higher costs.

POS are combined with a HMO or PPO to offer participants choice of selecting physicians outside of group of networked providers. The plans are usually coupled with an HMO or PPO, and requires more out of pocket expense if participants select a physician outside of the plan.

Location	Source	
Web	www.medicarerights.org www.catholiccharitiesusa.org	www.mcfa.gov www.medicare.gov
Agencies	**The Centers for Medicare and Medicaid Services (CMS)** 7500 Security Blvd. Baltimore, MD 21244 (800) MEDICARE (633-4227) (410) 786-3000 **Medicare Rights Center** 1460 Broadway, 11th Floor New York, NY 10036 (212) 869-3850 **Center of Health Care Rights** (800) 824-0780	**U.S. Department of Health & Human Services** P.O. Box 23489 Washington, DC 20026 (800) 447-8477 (Accepts Medical & Medicare Fraud Complaints) **Medicare Telephone Hot line** (800) 633-4227 (800) MEDICARE

Medical

Low-income persons who are in need of medical insurance can apply for Medical. Medical is a nation wide insurance payment plan for low-income persons and families. Numerous doctors accept Medical patients and almost all hospitals. Uninsured persons with low-incomes who have been hospitalized or anticipate being ill can apply for Medical coverage. Applications are available at Departments of Social Services offices. Caseworkers at hospitals also can assist patients with obtaining Medical.

Medicare

Medicare is federally operated to provide services to persons over the age of 65 and those with a disability that lasts 24 months or longer. Persons who are terminally ill, or no longer able to work due to a permanent disability can apply for medical regardless of their age. Caseworkers at hospitals assist patients with obtaining Medicare. For those facing a terminal illness the Medicare application can be expedited in order to cover current hospital costs and hospice fees. The Department of Heath and Human Services contracts with regional insurance companies to process claims. Medicare is divided into two parts: Part A for hospitalization costs and Part B covers medical costs.

Medigap

Medigap offers additional coverage to supplement costs that are not covered by Medicare. Persons interested in purchasing a Medigap plan should contact different providers to get the best price, as Medigap plans can be costly.

Location	Source
Web	www.ihealthcoalition.org www.mayohealth.org www.ama-assn.org www.healthfinder.org www.intelihealth.com www.unitedseniorshealth.org
Agencies	**United Seniors Health Council** 409 3rd Street, NW. Suite 200 Washington, DC 20024

Location	Source
	(800) 637-2604
	Insurance Information Institute 110 William Street New York, NY 10038 (212) 346-5500

OBTAINING HEALTH INSURANCE

Persons who do not have medical insurance, selecting a provider prior to an emergency is wise. With research obtaining medical insurance can be accomplished. The easiest route to obtaining prices for of health care is a health care insurance broker. Insurance brokers are able to provide several estimates and explain the provider's coverage's. Persons, who know which insurance provider they want, should contact the agency directly for enrollment.

In addition to standard medical care, there are many organizations, including the federal government, that provide free and/or low costs medical care for expecting mothers; the government provides access to a physician, nurse, and midwife, nurse practitioner, or often a team of health care professionals to assist with delivery of your child.

Location	Source
Books	Sack, Steven M. *The Working Women's Legal Survival Guide*. Prentice Hall Press, © 1998.
Web	www.hiaa.org www.insurance.com www.insweb.com www.intelliquote.com

Location	Source
	www.insure.com
	www.iii.org
Agencies	**Health Insurance Association Of America**
	1201 F Street, NW, 5th Floor
	Washington, DC 20004
	(202) 824-1600
	Insurance Information Institute
	110 William Street
	New York, NY 10038
	(212) 346-5500

Medical Broker

Medical insurance brokers work as independent agents for one or multiple providers. Most <u>do not</u> charge a fee for their services because they receive compensation from the medical provider once you enroll in a health care plan. A knowledgeable broker makes the search for insurance easy; they often prepare a form with the names of the providers who offer the type of coverage you desire along with the costs for each type of plan. Before selecting a plan, you may choose to obtain a report from different brokers before making a selection to compare the quality and costs of plans. In some instances, another broker may know of a comparable medical provider with competitive rates.

Location	Source
Web	www.ambest.com
	www.insweb.com
	www.quickquote.com
	www.1stquote.com
	www.instantquote.com

176

Location	Source
	http://worldwide-med.com

When looking for a medical broker you may want to ask a friend or co-worker for a referral. Most companies hire independent contractors who pay for their own medical coverage, often they can refer you to their broker.

Dental and Vision Insurance

Dental and vision insurance can be purchased with a health care plan or separately. Most Insurance brokers can prepare a quote that includes all the services that you desire. Dental and vision may be offered at no costs or at a reduced rate when purchasing health care coverage.

Location	Source
Web	www.bracesinfo.com www.insure.com www.captive.com www.ada.org
Agencies	**American Dental Association (ADA)** 211 East Chicago Avenue Chicago, IL 60611 (312) 440-2500

Health Care Providers

Health care providers now offer independent plans. With the number of contractors entering into the work force every year, there is a growing market for providing health care coverage to individuals. The providers and plans vary depending on the state. To begin, get the names of the most well-known and respected medical providers. Log onto their web site to find out if they provide individual plans. If you are unable to locate information on their web site, then send an e-mail to the contact person or customer support department. Most sites have a contact page where the company's telephone number and e-mail address are provided.

MEDICAL PRACTITIONERS

A knowledgeable practitioner is always researching solutions that are safe and proven for their patients. Practitioners are kept up to date on their patients care and continually seek the best treatment even if they refer their patients to other practitioners who specialize in the are of concern have proven successes. Locating practitioners of this caliber requires the combination of research, *luck*, and gut feelings. Many knowledgeable practitioners can be found throughout the country and there is help available for researching their background and learning about their successes. The following sections provide resources for several areas of practice.

Selecting a Practitioner

Different types of medical practitioners are available. Some practice traditional medical, some a combination of traditional and holistic, and others who solely rely on holistic remedies to cure. A set formula doest exist to selecting a *knowledgeable* practitioner; find someone with whom you're comfortable, has years of experience, sound knowledge of medical conditions and keeps you well informed of your options are key elements to identifying a practitioner.

Location	Source
Web	www.ffac.com www.afale.com www.pacificare.com www.healthnet.com

Chiropractor

Chiropractors practice a form of alternative treatment using touch and muscle stimulation to relieve pain. Chiropractors complete a thorough medical education before becoming licensed. Licensed and board certified chiropractors are commonly referred to as doctors. Some hospitals grant chiropractors the right to practice at their facility at the patient's request oftentimes along with the attending physician.

Location	Source
Web	www.chiro.org www.yourspine.com www.chiropractordirectory.com www.spine-health.com www.amerchiro.org
Agencies	**American Chiropractic Association (ACA)** 1701 Clarendon Blvd. Arlington, VA 22209 (800) 986-4636

Alternative Medical Care

Practitioners, including some physicians, whose practice is not to treat their patients with commercial drugs and surgeries are often referred to as holistic doctors. Holistic doctors use natural substances to cure patients and stress the importance of healthy diets. Treatment methods from holistic doctors isn't studied or measured against the performance of traditional physicians, so their success and failure treatment rates are unknown. The Food and Drug Administration (FDA) does not recognize most holistic treatments. Some hospitals grant hospital privileges to licensed holistic physicians and with the approval of the attending physician at the request of patients.

Location	Source	
Web	www.explorepub.com www.arxc.com www.altmedicine.com www.alternativemedicine.com www.litematters.com www.nccan.nih.gov www.herbplus.com	
Agency	**National Center for Complementary & Alternative Medicine** P.O. Box 7923 Gaithersburg, MD 20898 (888) 644-6226 (866) 464-3615	**Alternative Therapist** 2043 N. Berendo Los Angeles, CA 90022 (323) 663-7801

Traditional Physician

The most recognized practitioner is the traditional medical physician. Traditional physicians rely on commercial drugs and preferred methods to treat patients. Before dispensing,

180

only drugs that to be given to patients must meet FDA approval, this rule applies to drugs used in study programs. Medical insurance plans almost always cover the costs for physician fees. Customarily traditional physicians network with other doctors and are members of various medical boards to ensure they are kept up-to-date on medical alternatives for their patients.

Location	Source	
Web	www.docsonline.com www.ama-assn.org	
Agencies	**American Academy Of Dermatology (AAD)** 930 N. Meacham Road Schaumburg, IL 60173-4965 (888) 330-0230 **American Academy of Family Physicians (AAFP)** 11400 Tomahawk Creek Parkway Leawood, KS 66201 (800) 274-2237	**American Medical Association** 515 North State Street Chicago, IL 60610 (800) 621-8335

RESEARCHING A DOCTORS BACKGROUND

We all have heard horrific stories about physicians leaving sponges inside patients and amputating the wrong leg. While these stories may be true they are not commonplace. With the number of people who are ill and require medical attention, a small percentage of patients encounter negligent treatment from physicians. Knowledgeable physicians do exist, but unfortunately there are bad ones too. Resources are available to help patients research a doctor's background, become aware of complaints from other patients and find out if legal action was taken for misconduct even murder. State medical boards can provide this information free of charge, many states have online forms for filing complaints.

Location	Source	
Web	www.checkbook.org	
Agencies	**U.S. Department of Health and Human Services** OIG Hotline P.O. Box 17303 Baltimore, MD 21203-7303	**Center for the Study of Services** 733 15th Street, NW Washington, DC 20005 (202) 347-7283
	U.S. Department of Health and Human Services Health Care Financing Administration 7500 Security Blvd. Baltimore, MD 21244	

Filing a Complaint Against a Practitioner

Patients who have experienced adverse medical treatment have the option of filing a complaint with the state board that license medical practitioners. Patients who have suffered injuries at the hands of negligent practitioners also can file a medical malpractice suit, for more information *see the Malpractice section below.* Most states have web sites that allow persons to file complaints online. It's important to document the date the behavior or injury occurred, include copies of the medical charts that document the injury (request copies of your medical chart from the hospital or medical office before filing a complaint), patients have a right to complete copy of their file.

Malpractice

Medical malpractice consists of the improper or negligent treatment of a patient that results in injury, loss or damage. The requirements for medical malpractice vary by state. Consult with a knowledgeable attorney regarding the legal requirements in your state. Obtain a copy of your medical records dating back 10 years (you may be ask to show proof that the sponge didn't jump into your stomach). Get information from hospital personnel, they may know of past complaints and lawsuits against the accused doctor. Outline the events as they occurred and organize the documentation so that your time with the attorney is fully utilized; in addition, ask the attorney what documentation you need to bring prior to the meeting. Some states do not record malpractice suites under a certain dollar amount; consult with an experienced malpractice attorney for more information regarding your state laws.

Location	Source	
	Lasko, Matthew. *Free Legal Help*. Made E-Z Products, Inc., © 2001.	Naifeh, Steven and Gregory White Smith. *The Best Lawyers In America.*
Book	Jasper, Margaret C. *Law of Medical Malpractice* Oceana Publications © 1996.	Woodward/White, Inc., © 2000.

Location	Source
Web	www.lawguru.com www.hcfa.gov www.uslaw.com
Agency	**U.S. Department of Health and Human Service** Office of Civil Rights 330 Independence Ave., SW Room 5250 Washington, DC 20201

LOW/NO COST MEDICAL CARE

Many people do not qualify for public assistance, yet they cannot afford the costs of medical treatments. Organizations have been formed to support patients with certain injuries, diseases, and virus; these organizations offer free or low costs medical treatment. In addition, some physicians waive co-payment fees for patients who have limited incomes. For more information on locating low or no costs medical care refer to the following resources.

Location	Source	
Web	www.hrsa.gov/osp/dfcr www.aoanet.org www.aircareall.org	www.patient.org www.patientravel.org
Agencies	**Hill-Barton Program** **Free Hospital** (800) 638-0742 **Association of** **Healthcare Medical**	**Offices of Minority** **Health Resources** P.O. Box 37337 Washington DC 20013-7337 (800) 444-6472

Location	Source

Lawyers

Healthcare Advocator's
5145 Yarmouth Ave.,
Suite 2
Encino, CA 91316
(818) 705-3059

**Health Resources and
Services Administration**
Department of Health and
Human services
Division of Facilities
Compliance and Recovery
Medical Care Program
5600 Fisher Lane, Room
10C-16
Rockville, MD 20857

**U.S. Department of
Health and Human
Services Administration**
Rockville, MD 20857
(800) 638-0742

**Mercy Care
Corporation**
2424 Vista Way, Suite
204
Oceanside, CA 92054
(888) 776-3729

Angel Flight (West)
3237 Donald Douglas
Loop South
Santa Monica, CA
90405
(888) 426-2643
(Travel for medical
treatment)

ADDITIONAL RESOURCES

The following is additional information on health care subjects covered in this guide.

Location	Source	
Web	www.ihs.gov www.hispanichealth.org www.americanmenopause.org www.lupus.org	www.aad.org www.ahrq.gov www.healthlaw.org
Agencies	**Indian Health Services** Parkdawn Bldg., Room 6-35 5600 Fisher Lane Rockville, MD 20857 (301) 443-3593 **American Menopause Foundation (AMF)** 350 Fifth Avenue, Suite 2822 New York, NY 10118 (212) 714-2398 **Mercy Medical Air Lift / National Patient Travel Center** (800) 296-1217 **American Academy Of Dermatology (AAD)** 930 North Meacham Road Schaumburg, IL 60173-4965 (888) 462-3376 **National Alliance For Hispanic Health**	**Office of Minority Health Resources** P.O. Box 37337 Washington, DC 2001-7337 (800) 444-6472 **National Health Information Center** P.O. Box 1133 Washington, DC 20013-1133 (800) 336-4797 **Lupus Foundation of America** 1300 Picard Drive, Suite 200 Rockville, MD 20850-4303 (800) 558-0121 **Agency For Health Care Research & Quality (AHRQ)** Publications Clearing House

Location	Source
	1501 16th Street, NW P.O. Box 8547

1501 16th Street, NW   P.O. Box 8547
Washington, DC 20036   Silver Spring, MD
(202) 387-5000   20907-8547
                      (800) 358-9295

Air Lifeline
(877) Air-Life

Chapter 7

Renting, Leasing, Purchasing and Refinancing Property

If I were asked to name the chief benefit of the house, I should say: the house shelters day-dreaming, the house protects the dreamer, the house allows one to dream in peace.
Gaston Bachelard

W eather it's the first time out on your own and you need help on where to begin, or you're considering purchasing a home, interested in renting or leasing a property, or homeless; help is available.

☼How The Information Was Found

The information contained in this chapter came primarily from personal experience and resources collected over the years. Before attempting to rent, lease, purchase or refinance property, ensure that the agent thoroughly explains the process, go as far as having them put it in writing.

Books can provide helpful pointers to first time buyers and sellers alike. For those buying a home and representing yourself the best resource is a helpful and knowledgeable escrow agent and college bookstores. Look for extension courses on obtaining a real-estate license, you may find valuable information to help you make a wise purchase and secure a comfortable loan.

PURCHASING A HOME

Purchasing a home is a universal nightmare that escapes no first time buyer. Becoming a homeowner is as achievable as purchasing a car, although there is more paper work and additional *hoops* to jump through. Similarly there are sales people and, for most of us, financing companies · which should begin to turn most stomachs. Although this should not be the case when one thinks of buying a house, but it is the inevitable reality

Where to Begin

For those who need to finance the purchase of a home the first step is to determine how much house one can qualify for before looking for a property.

The first step to purchasing a home is obtaining copies of credit reports from the three major credit report agencies:

Experian
P.O. Box 9595
Allen, TX 75013
(800) 583-4080
(800) 397-3742
(800) Experian

Trans Union
P.O. Box 2000
Chester, PA 19022
(800) 916-8800

Equifax
P.O. Box 740241
Atlanta, GA 30374
(800) 882-0648

If turned down for credit within the past 6 months the report is free of charge.

Two methods exist for consideration when purchasing a home.

1. If one has at least 20% down then purchasing is possible even with marginal credit. In addition, you can receive the best interest rates available.

2. If one has a *good* (A-A+) credit rating, then purchasing is possible even with no money down.

Buying a home with or without using a real-estate agent

Laws don't require homebuyers to use a real-estate agent when purchasing or selling a home. Prospective home buyers can locate their desired residence, secure financing, and negotiate the purchase terms without the assistance of an agent.

American Society of Home Inspectors
www.ashi.com

Home Appraisals
www.appraisalinstitute.org

Locating help for buying a home without an agent is difficult. Colleges that offer extension courses in real estate licensing sell books for enrolled students on purchasing real estate. A couple of web-sites are available, but the information scarce. The following list was compiled when I purchased my first home after choosing the cities foremost incompetent real-estate agent. I created the list to ensure that my next purchase went smoothly. The list applies mainly to the state of California; apply the steps pertinent to your state. A knowledgeable attorney or escrow agent can be of further assistance.

- Locate financing options

- Locate the desired property
- A *good faith* deposit is made to ensure that the purchase is legitimate. The money is applied to the down payment on the house or is refunded if sell does not go through
- Submit an offer/counter offers (negotiate your terms)
- Acceptance of the offer
- Establish an agreement with the seller's agent (if there is one) to receive a portion of the commission as you are acting as your own agent (for home buyers only).
- Open Escrow (whichever party selects the escrow company opens the escrow). Ensure a date that both parties agree upon is established for the close of escrow. The closing date drives the purchase of the home, but is, in many cases, easily extended. If an extension occurs, then ensure that a new date is set IN WRITING and not a guesstimate
- Arrange a home inspection. The home inspection typically occurs within 10 days of the acceptance of the offer, depending on the terms of your contract and escrow documents. If you are traveling out of town ensure that the date meets your schedule
- Obtain a property profile. The title company that you select can provide a preliminary title report at no charge. Since you are representing yourself, negotiate with the seller's agent to allow the option to either select the title company or escrow agency. Both the sellers and buyers pay escrow and title fees so the selection should be 50/50
- The title company typically can provide both the sellers and buyers with a preliminary title report delineating any liens, easements, mortgages and/or modifications to the title of the house
- Sign a contract between the seller and buyer
- Seller provides buyer with disclosure documents that provide detailed information on the condition of the home, which they must disclose all defects; they also must notify the buyer if the house is in a flood zone, fire hazard area, or chemical hazardous environment

- The buyer at this time should secure financing
- The buyer's lending company requests a home inspection once the financing is secured, this typically occurs within 10 days of the loan documents approval
- The sellers must have a termite inspection on the property and present a copy to the buyer prior to the close of escrow
- The buyer demands all necessary repairs in writing.
- Final walk though – ensure necessary repairs have been made and that all terms met
- The buyer financing company will fund the loan
- Buyer and sellers sign escrow documents
- Receive keys the day of signing unless otherwise stipulated in your escrow documents

Location	Source
Book	Tazer, Milt. *How To Buy or Sell Your Home Without A Broker.* Prentice Hall Press, © 2000. *Do-it-Yourself Kit Buying/Selling Your Home Made E-Z Kits.* Made E-Z Products, Inc. Sendell, Kathleen. *The Unofficial Guide to Buying a Home Online* by. IDG Books Worldwide, Inc., © 2000. Glink, Ilyce K. *100 Questions Every First-Time Home Buyer Should Ask. 2nd Edition.* Time Books, © 2000.
Web	www.home-buyer-seller-tips.com www.realtylocator.com www.homeseekers.com www.americas-real-estate.com www.ads4homes.com www.bestagents.com www.newhomes.net www.mortgagemag.com www.debtworkout.com www.realtor.com www.owners.com

Location	Source
	www.newhomenetwork.com
Agencies	**HUD Housing Counseling Clearing House** (888) 466-3487

Selecting a Real-Estate Agent

The foremost quality a real estate agent must possess is experience! Competent real-estate agents must be able to provide you with a list of items you need to complete as well as overview of what to expect; they must introduce you to several lenders if you have not secured financing on your own. The agent should be knowledgeable and keep you abreast on the purchase or sale of your home – a true professional.

The best method for locating a real estate agent is referral from a close friend or relative. Everybody knows somebody who's a real estate agent, but you don't want any body, you want the best, as the purchase of a home is a huge investment of finances and time. The next preferred method is to call an agency. Most agencies have real estate agents answering the telephones, so if an inquirer calls they can immediately make arrangements to meet with the person. If you don't like the person or they are unable to answer questions satisfactorily, then hang up and call back later to find someone who seems competent.

Home Refinancing

Home refinancing is a less *greasier* than the initial home purchase and the experience gained from purchasing a home becomes handy. The major concern for person desiring to refinance is obtaining the lowest points (if any) and a low monthly interest rate.

What are points?

Points are percentages of the loan amount to be paid by the borrower(s) to the bank and/or broker for giving you the loan (this is additional the interest they charge for you taking the loan). Banks, brokers and lenders can charge points on loans. For example a loan for $110,000 with 2 points the borrower(s) pays $2,200 plus additional closing costs. It's wise to search for loans that have low or no points. A familiar phrase for mortgage brokers is I could charge you up to seven points, but I'm only charging you three. Anything greater than 1-½ points is a considerable amount for a loan, unless the interest rate is low. A cleaver borrower should reply, *You can charge me a million points if I can't pay three I can't pay a million.*

Location	Source	
Web	www.homemakers.com	www.bankrate.com
	www.homeowners.com	www.e-law.com
	www.keystrck.com	www.fanniemae.com
	www.mortgagemag.com	www.fhlbanks.com
	www.debtworkout.com	

Selling a Home

After weathering the home purchase and possible refinancing it's time to sell. Many people are reluctant to leave their castle, but the average time a person owns a home is between five to seven years. Depending on the economy, sellers have the most say in how the property transaction occurs. Because the seller is responsible for paying the real estate agent commissions in addition to closing cost their interest tends be highly regarded.

Selling a Home Without Using Real-Estate Agent

As with purchasing a home, selling a house does not require the assistant of a real estate agent. Consider the seller the party responsible for paying commission to real-estate agents, which these fees can be as high as 6% depending on the laws with your state. If your home sells for $375,000 then you pay the closing cost fees, inspection cost in addition to a commission one can pay well over $25,000 to sell their home. For many *For Sell By Owner* is the only way to sell.

Unlike home purchases, there are many resources for sellers who choose not utilize a real estate agent. With the use of the Internet sellers can post their property online to attract buyers. In addition, there are books available to homeowners who want to sell their property themselves.

Location	Source
Books	Carey, Bill, Chantal Howell and Suzanne Kiffmann. *How To Sell Your Home Without a broker 3rd Edition.* John Wiley & Sons Inc, © 2000. *Do-it-Yourself Kit Buying/Selling Your Home Made E-Z Kits.* Made E-Z Products, Inc. Eilers, Terry. *How To Sell Your Home Fast.* © 1997.
Web	www.fsbconnection.com www.fsbosites.com www.owners.com www.fsboworld.net www.yourfsbo.com www.fsbotips.com www.fsbonetwork.com

RENTING/LEASING PROPERTY

Renting is similar to leasing except for the terms time the tenancy. Renting is typically short-term no more than 12 months and is often month-to-month until either party terminates the agreement. Leasing is a predefined period of time stated within the contract. Some persons choose to lease for many of years. A lease is typically renewed every 12 months for another 12-month period. Real-estate agents or brokers are a useful source to finding property for prospective tenants. Those who want to know more about rent control and other restrictions can contact the state housing authority for more information.

Location	Source
Web	www.rent.net
	www.aptsforrent.com
	www.rentcheck.com
	www.hud.gov/renting/index.cfm
	www.roommatelocator.com

Landlord Tenant Disputes/ Evictions

Communication is the key to finding resolution with conflicts. If one party is unwilling to communicate, then taking your dispute to an arbitrator or judge becomes the only means for resolving differences. The resources below offer hints and suggestions for resolving differences between landlords and tenants; these resources are less expensive than attorney and court fees.

Tenants who are being served eviction notices have several legal recourses to assist with receiving a fair hearing. Each state has requirements on how an eviction is to transpire, this information is also available online as well as forms to complete for court filings. Tenants often succeed at staying an *illegal* eviction, which affords the tenant additional time to locate alternative housing. Fighting an eviction on your own often proves to be as effective as a hiring an attorney. Spend a few hours in the law library to familiarize yourself with legal terms. Books in law libraries, and in some public libraries, provide sample forms on what to file along with clear explanations as to their purpose. The law protects those who are facing evictions as a result of racial discrimination; these cases are often heard in a superior or federal court.

Location	Source
Books	Portman, Janet . Marcia Stewart, Ralph Warner. *Every Landlord's Legal Guide.* Nolo Press © 2001. Portman, Janet . Marcia Stewart. *Every Tenant's Legal Guide.* Nolo Press © 1999. Portman, Janet . Marcia Stewart. *Renters' Rights: The Basics.* Nolo Press © 2002.
Web	www.tenant.net www.attyfind.com www.lawguru.com http://aptrentersresource.com www.nolo.com
Agencies	**U.S. Department of Housing and Urban Development Office of Investigation** 451 7th Street, SW., Room 5208 Washington, DC 24010-2000 (800) 669-9777

HOUSING FOR RUNAWAY TEENAGERS

Numerous factors contribute to a teenager leaving home without notifying parents of their whereabouts. Some teenagers suffer physical and emotional abuses so intolerable that locating alternative housing becomes a must for survival; help is available for those teenagers. Often times schools locate housing to ensure that the child is able to continue their education and live in a less threatening environment.

In turn some teenager runaways believe others are treated better, receive more *things* and have parents who pay attention to their every needs. A standardize method for parenting doesn't exist, every household is different yet there are some similarities that tie all of us together. Teens must understand that everyone is different including members in their home. It's important for teenagers to know that some parents over compensate by giving their children things that they never had; the child grows up spoiled and unemployable.

For teenagers who have left home and need help on locating a place to live the following resources are available:

Location	Source	
Web	www.child.net www.standforkids.org www.calib.com	
Agencies	**Covenant House Nineline** 346 W. 17th Street New York, NY 10011 (800) 999-9999 **National Youth Cases Line** (800) 448-4663 **National Center Poverty Law**	**Children of the Night** (800) 551-1300 (800) 999-9915 TDD/TYY **National Runaway Switch Board** (800) 621-4000 (800) 621-0394 (TDD)

Location	Source
	205 West Monroe Street Chicago, IL 60606 (312) 263-3830

LOCATING LOW-INCOME AND GOVERNMENT SUBSIDIZED HOUSING

Finding low-income or government subsidized housing no longer requires the skills of a professional social worker. Apartment complexes throughout the country offer special rates to those who are low-income, in addition; the Housing and Urban Development (HUD) department website contains valuable information for persons with little or no income who need shelter; they also offer emergency shelter programs for those who are homeless.

Location	Source	
Web	www.us.dhhs.gov www.povertylaw.org www.hud.gov www.communityactionpartnership.com www.habitat.org	
Agencies	**Community Action Partnership** 1100 17th St., NW. Suite 500 Washington, DC 20036 **US Department of Housing and Urban Development** 451 7th Street, SW Washington, DC	**U.S. Department of Health & Human Services** P.O. Box 23489 Washington, DC 20026 (800) 447-8477 **Habitat For Humanity** Partner Service Center 121 Habitat Street Americus, GA 31709 (229) 924-6935 ext.

Location	Source	
	20410	2551 or 2552
	(202) 708-1112	
	National Low Income Housing Coalition (NLIHC) 1012 Fourteenth Street NW, Suite 610 Washington, D.C. 20005 (202) 662-1530	

HOMELESS

In addition to the resources for low-income persons the following resources are geared to those who are homeless and desire shelter.

Location	Source	
Web	www.nchannet www.nchari.net www.nationalhomerless.org	www.nlchp.org www.efsp.unitedway.org www.nlihc.org
Agencies	**National Coalition for the Homeless** 1012 Fourteenth Street, NW, #600, Washington, DC 20005-3471 (202) 737-6444 **The National Law Center on Homelessness & Poverty** 1411 K Street NW, Suite 1400 Washington, DC 20005 (202) 638-2535	**Emergency Food/Shelter National Board Program** 701 North Fairfax Street Suite 310 Alexandria, VA 22314-2064 (703) 706-9660 **National Low Income Housing Coalition**

Location	Source
	(NLIHC) 1012 Fourteenth Street NW, Suite 610 Washington, D.C. 20005 (202) 662-1530

First Time On Your Own

You can survive independent living – it really isn't so difficult as long as you have a job or lots of available money saved. Yes there will be downs at the beginning but if you keep working you'll prevail and success is forthcoming. An essential part of independent living is obtaining a place to live, this is a defining skill for adults. Several options are available for obtaining shelter, other than relaying on mom and dad; they are renting/leasing, rooming (renting a room), or purchasing property. Other options exist such as joining the military or living in a shelter, but many choose to make it on their own before relying on those sources. Finding a place to live isn't as difficult as it seems. With some research and a little help, independent living can be achieved.

Colleges typically have a list of places to rent rooms provided by residents who live near the campus (some schools post this information online). The college can also put you in contact with other students looking for roommates to share the high costs of attending college and living independently. Research all of your options and use the information provided in the above sections. From experience I can assure that living independently is a huge step but it's not impossible.

Chapter 8

Consumer Advocacy

We cannot safely leave politics to politicians,
or political economy to college professors.
The people themselves must think, because the
people alone can act.

Henry George

With the number of agencies that report negative information as well as personal information it's hard to believe that there is help for the common man/woman.

☼How The Information Was Found

You may notice that there are few, if any, consumer advocacy sections in the bookstores, libraries, and online. The lack of clear direction to finding information to protect your rights is not difficult by employing some thought. If you're searching for information online, then summarize what you are looking for into phrases. For example, locating help online for information battling a car mechanic over a poor work. Search for resources that include phrases like automotive fraud, mechanical fraud, or automotive agencies. Depending on the search engines the results may be enormous, continue to sort from the list provided until the desired information if found.

WHERE TO FILE A COMPLAINT

All companies are required to uphold standard business practices and ethics governed by both the state and federal governments. With so many agencies, knowing where to file a complaint is key.

The consumer has the final say as he/she can opt not to support a company financially by patronizing another establishment. Various reports state that consumers tell at lest 10 people of a bad experience. With newspapers and *consumer watchdog* television, one can reach millions. Consumers are regularly defrauded, deceived, and exploited. Ways to protect your rights are available and information contained in this chapter is designed to help people to find on how to fight back!

Location	Source	
Books	Lesko, Matthew. *Free Legal Help*. Made E-Z Products, Inc. © 2001. Kramon, James M., Esq. *You Don't Need a Lawyer*. © 2002.	
Web	www.fraud.org www.consumer.gov www.fic.org www.cftc.gov	www.mojones.com www.speakout.com www.politicalindex.com
Agencies	**FCC (Federal Communications Commission)** Common Carrier Bureau Consumer Complaints Mail Stop 1600A2 Washington, DC 20554	**FTC (Federal Trade Commission)** Consumer Response Center Washington, DC 20580 (877) FTC-HELP (382-4357) **US Postal Inspection Services**

Location	Source	
	FTC Identity Theft Hotline (877) ID Theft (438-4338)	(800) 654-8896 (For fraud and illegal activities using the US Postal System)
	Commodity Futures Trading Commission 3 Lafayette Center 1155 21st Street, NW Washington, DC 20581	**National Fraud Information Center** (800) 876-7060

Opt out from mailing list is offered by credit reporting agencies:
(888) 5OPTOUT
(888) 567-8688 and DMA (Direct Marketing Association)

CREDIT CARD FRAUD

Anyone experiencing problems with credit cards should immediately contact their bank in writing send (letter certified mailed or via fax). The bank has to initiate an investigation according to the Fair Credit Billing Act enforced by the Federal Trade Commission (FTC); they send you a bill minus those charges until their investigation is completed. Notify then bank in writing disputing their practice if the bank has failed to follow the laws and at the same time contact the FTC to file a formal complaint.

Location	Source
Books	Strong, Howard. *What Every Credit Card User Needs to Know: How To Protect yourself and*

Location	Source
	Your Money. Owl Books © 1999.
Web	www.nat/consumersleague.org www.ftc.gov www.mmintl.org www.fraud.org
Agencies	**FTC (Federal Trade Commission)** Consumer Response Center Washington, DC 20580 (877) FTC-HELP (382-4357) FTC Identity Theft Hotline (877) ID Theft (438-4338)	**National Consumers League** 1701 K Street, NW. Suite 1200 Washington, DC 20006 (800) 876-7060 (202) 835-3323

LOAN FRAUD

All financial institutions are licensed by the state. Persons should first send the institution a written notice of fraud, via letter, documenting the type of fraud they committed how they can resolve the problem without escalating to the state and federal agencies. Depending on the response, persons have the option of filing a complaint with the licensing agency of the state (oftentimes called the comptroller office) and retaining a knowledgeable attorney to recovery cost and punitive damages.

Location	Source
Web	www.nclnet.org www.fraud.org www.consumersinterests.org www.scambusters.com
	Alliance Against Fraud in **Federal Deposit**

Location	Source	
Agencies	**Telemarketing and Electronic Commerce (AAFTEC)** 1701 K. Street, NW. Suite 1200 Washington, DC 20006 (202) 835-3323 **American Council on Consumer Interests (ACCI) Columbia, MO 65211** (573) 882-3817 **Consumer Alert** 1001 Connecticut Ave, NW Suite 1128 Washington, DC 20036 (202) 467-5809	**Insurance Corporation** 25 Ecker St., Suite 1600 San Francisco, CA 94105 **National Credit Union Administration** 2300 Clayton Road, Suite 1350 Concord, CA 94520 (925) 363-6200

CONSUMER AGENCIES

The following are resources to the major consumer protection agencies that are located nationwide. States consumer agencies are also available and oftentimes more efficiently at resolving disputes, so it is wise to contact both government bodies.

Location	Sources	
Web	www.checkbook.org www.consumerreports.org www.the-dma.org www.sec.gov www.healthprivacy.org www.nclnet.org www.consumeralert.org www.consumerinterests.org www.bbb.org	www.Fraud.org www.carsdirect.com www.scrambusters.com www.autobytel.com www.fda.gov. www.womenautohelp.com www.angryconsumer.com www.kellybluebook.com www.pueblo.ssa.gov

Location	Sources
	www.notice.com www.autobuyingtips.com www.aclu.org www.consumerlawpage.com www.theautostop.com www.edmends.com www.cpsc www.ftc.gov www.pueblo.gsa.gov www.corpwatch.org www.checkfraud.org www.prig.org www.nclnet.org www.healthprivacy.org
Agencies	**Institute For Health Care Research and Policy** 2233 Wisconsin Avenue, NW Suite 525 Washington, DC 20007 (202) 687-0880 **American Civil Liberties Union (ACLU)** 1400 20th St., NW, Suite 119 Washington, DC 20036 Tel.: (202) 457-0800 (Washington DC Office) **Better Business Bureau Auto Hotline** 4200 Wilson Blvd. Suite 800 Arlington, VA 22203-1804 (800) 955-5100 **Center for Auto Safety** (All Major Auto Manufacturers) 1825 Connecticut Ave. NW Washington, DC 20009 (202) 328-7700 **Federal Consumer Information Center (FCIC)** **Consumer Alert** 1001 Connecticut Avenue, NW Suite 1128 Washington, DC (202) 467-5809 **Alliance Against Fraud In Telemarketing and Electronic Commerce (AAFTEC)** 1701 K. Street, NW Suite 1200 Washington, DC 20006 (202) 835-3323 **American Council on Consumer Interest (ACCI)** 240 Stanley Hall US Securities and Exchange Commission (SEC) 450 Fifth Street, NW Washington, DC 20549-0213 (202) 942-7040 (800) SEC-0330 **DMA (Direct Marketing Association)** Consumer Affairs 1111 19th Street, NW

Pueblo, CO 81009
(800) 688-9889
TTY (800) 326-2996

Suite 1100
Washington, DC 20036
(202) 955-5030

Center for the Study of Services
733 15th Street, NW
Washington, DC 20025
(202) 347-7283

Opt Out From Mailing List Offered by Credit Reporting
Agencies
(888) 5OPTOUT
(888) 675-8688

Consumer Union of US (CU)
101 Truman Avenue
Yonkers, NY 10703-1057
(914) 378-2000

AUTOMOTIVE FRAUD

Anyone who has purchased a car or taken one in for service understands that the automotive industry is an incubator for criminals. Both men and women are defrauded out of millions of dollars from bad car purchase deals or shoddy repairs. Collectively people must act to put an end to this blatant robbery. For persons who have experienced problems, the first attempt is to resolve differences with the car manufacturer directly instead of the dealership, who often sees misfortune as a green light to sell you another automobile. If all fails, then take your complaint public as these manufacturers rely on naive people to purchase their transportation.

Location	Source	
Web	www.womenautohelp.com	www.bbb.org
	www.nada.org	www.nhtfa.dov.gov
	Automotive Consumer	**Council of Better**

Location	Source	
Agencies	**Action Program (AUTOCAP)** 8400 West Park Dr. McLean, VA 22102 (703) 821-7000 (800) 252-6232	**Business Bureaus, Inc. (BBB Auto Line)** 4200 Wilson Blvd, Suite 800 Arlington, VA 22203-1838
	National Highway Traffic Safety Administration U.S. department of Transportation 400 7th Street ,SW, Room 20590 Washington, DC 20590 (800) 424-9393	(703) 276-0100 (800) 276-0100

BEING HEARD

Getting the attention you need to air a dispute is often difficult. Many news stations have consumer reporters who air disputes with major companies within their area. Try contacting your local paper in addition to taking out an advertisement detailing the dispute, as the advertisement cost is inexpensive (for small town papers) and could reach thousands depending on the circulation size. Another effective avenue is posting comments online or creating a website that delineates your problem.

Location	Source
Book	Kramon, James M., Esq. *You Don't Need a Lawyer.* © 2002.
Web	www.angryconsumer.com www.consumers-action.org www.consumerfed.org

Location	Source
	www.consumeralert.org www.callforaction.org www.consumer-action.org
Agencies	**National Credit Union Admin. (NCUA)** 2300 Clayton Rd., Suite 1350 Concord, CA 94520 (925) 363-6200 **Federal Deposit Insurance Corporation (FDIC)** Compliance & Consumer Affairs San Francisco, CA 94105 (415) 546-0160 **Federal Communications Commission Complaints** 2025 m Street NW, Suite 8210 Washington, DC 20554 (888) 225-5322	**Consumers Union of U.S.** 101 Truman Ave. Yonkers, NY 10703 (914) 378- 200 (800) 234-1645 **Consumer Action** 717 Market Street, Suite 310 San Francisco, CA 94103 (415) 777-9635 (415) 777-9456 (TTY) (213) 623-8327 (Hot Line) **Consumer Federation of America (CFA)** 1424 16th Street, NW, Suite 604 Washington, DC 20036 (202) 387-6121 **Call for Action, Inc** 5272 River Rd. Suite 300 Bethesda, MD 20816 (301) 657-7490 (301) 657-9462 (TTY)

TELEMARKETERS

Who hasn't been interrupted by the annoying calls from telemarketers? Telemarketing is the largest telephone annoyance persons face, but it is effective. Small businesses are around because of their success at telemarketing. You would be amazed at the amount of personal information some consumers disclose over the telephone. Stop disclosing information and they will stop calling.

Location	Source	
Web	www.ftc.org www.fraud.org www.consumer-action.org	
Agencies	**National Consumers League** 1701 K Street NW, Suite 1200 Washington, DC 20006 (800) 876-7060 (202) 853-3323 **Federal Information Center** (800) 688-9889	**U.S. Postal Inspection Service** 475 L'Enfant Plaza, SW Washington, DC 20260-2100 (800) 654-8896 (Fraud Hotline)

Removing your name from Marketing List

Call:
Experian: (800) 228-4571 ext. 5247
Haines Criss & Coss/Americalist
(800) 850-9558
Sub Trans Union (888) 567-8688

CLASS ACTION LAWSUITS

After becoming fed up with poor, negligently and unlawful behavior, individuals may exercise their right to file a lawsuit against companies who have no regard for the law, and repeatedly use their position to take advantage of consumers. Class action lawsuits typically involve suits involving a large number of people with similar legal claims.

The individuals join together in a group (the class) to sue usually a company or organization. For more information regarding class action lawsuits consult the following resources:

Location	Source	
Web	www.notice.com	www.classaction.com
	www.consumerlaw.org	www.lawguru.com
	www.classactionamerica.com	www.bigclassaction.com

Chapter 9

Financial Problems and Repair

Thy fate is the common fate of all;
Into each life some rain must fall.
Henry Wadsworth Longfellow

P eople experience problems. Do not be discouraged when you're experiencing difficulties, relax as it is temporary. When I face difficult struggles I often recite to myself the phrase *this too shall pass* and in a while it does. Persons needing help to repair their lives and/or finances should take comfort in knowing that help is available.

☼How The Information Was Found

When it comes to locating consumer credit counselors (CCCs) you will have only one problem, which one to choose. Consumer credit counselors, who work on behalf of credit companies to negotiate the bills, write thousands of web resources and hundreds of books, but were not included (unless one slipped in) because this book is designed to empower individuals.

Having made that clear, the resources for this section were slim pickings. Although there are many resources in this chapter, they were added over time by researching web sites, bookstores, and attending seminars, and because of time constraints, this chapter was almost removed.

CREDIT PROBLEMS AND REPAIR

The major problem with credit reporting is the underground world of credit repair services. A person can serve seven years for attempted murder, but a debtor is punished for not paying bills on time for twice as many years. Negotiating payments with creditors is an option for many people to quickly end disputes with creditors. The following resources are available to people who need assistance with repairing their credit.

Location	Source	
Books	Bill, Kelly Jr. *The Complete Guide to Credit Repair:* Adams Media Corporation, © 2001. McWhorter, Jember Brette. Attorney at Law. *Repair Your Own Credit and Deal with Debt:* Sphinx Publishing, © 2001.	Ventura, John. *The Credit Repair Kit.* Dearborn, © 1998. Pilot, Kevin. *Credit Approved.* Adam Media Corporation, © 1992.
Web	www.mmintl.org/hotline/dealing.htm www.armchairmillionaire. com www.ramresearch.com www.ncua.org www.consumer-action.org www.getsmart.com www.debt.help.com www.FDIC.gov www.debtworkout.com	
Agencies	**Federal Deposit Insurance Corporation (Bank Complaints)** 25 Ecker Street, Suite 1600 San Francisco, CA 94105 Public Reference Room 130 Federal Trade Commission	**National Credit Union Administration** 2300 Clayton Road, Suite 1350 Concord, CA 94520 (925) 363-6200

Location	Source
	Washington, DC 20580 (877) FTC-Help (202) 326-2222

IRS AUDITS

The IRS has a reputation for being the last agency anyone wants to encounter. This reputation is well earned as for many years citizens have been financially destroyed at the hands of collecting IRS agents. Persons facing problems with the IRS must understand their rights; oftentimes the IRS makes errors that prove to be advantageous to taxpayers. For those whose paths have crossed with the IRS the following resources are available:

Location	Source	
Books	Goldstein, Arnold S. *How to Settle With the Irs--For Pennies on the Dollar* Garrett Pub © 1997. Minns, Michael Louis. *How to Survive the IRS: My Battles Against Goliath* Ron Paul Barricade Books © 2001.	Estill, Scott M. *Tax This!: An Insider's Guide to Standing Up to the IRS* Self Counsel Press © 2000.
Web	www.Consumerwatchdog.org www.uslaw.com/problem.tcl?problem_id=127	
Agency	**Problem Resolution Staff** Internal Revenue Service	

Location	Source
	U.S. Department of the Treasury
	1111 Constitution Ave., NW, Room 1027
	Washington, DC 20224
	(800) 829-1040

BILL COLLECTORS

The FTC (Federal Trade Commission) has enacted the Fair Debt Collection Practices Act to address the concerns of consumers who are harassed by collection agencies. In addition many people have successfully sued collection agencies for their illegal practices. Persons who are being harassed should notify the collection agency can consider the following resources:

Location	Source
Web	www.ftc.gov (Fair Debt Collection Practices Act)
Agencies	**Credit and Your Consumer Rights and Fair Debt Collection** Consumer Response Center Federal Trade Commission CRC-240 Washington, DC 20580 (877) FTC-HELP

BANKRUPTCY

Deciding to file for bankruptcy could be the beginning to living a debt free life. It's common for persons to state that once they file for bankruptcy they were able to manage their finances better. Bankruptcy is not the first choice for many as it doesn't erase negative reporting from the credit bureaus and may not relieve persons of all their debts.

Before considering bankruptcy make a list of debts that you are certain you cannot repay; and a second list of accounts you're willing to settle with creditors (after a bankruptcy has been filed petitioners can reopen their case to add items). Proceed with the bankruptcy knowing your strengths and desired outcome.

Location	Resources
Books	Kevin, Pilot. *Credit Approved.* Adam Media Corporation, © 1992. Sommer, Henry J. *The Complete Guide To Chapter 7 and Chapter 13.* © 1994.
Web	http:// bankrupt.com www.abiworld.org http:/creditscoring.com www.law.cornell.edu/topics/bankruptcy.html http://nacba.com/ www.debtworkout.com www.consumer-action.org
Agencies	**American Bankruptcy Institute** Info@abiworld.org (email) **NACBA (National Association of Consumer Bankruptcy Attorneys) National Headquarters** 2300 M St., N.W. Suite 800 Washington, D.C. 20037 (202) 331-8005 (202) 331-8535 fax

Automobile Repossessions

Vehicle loans have a clause that makes the lender the lien holder until the debt is paid in full plus any interest that applies. Lenders typically place a lean on the automobile to ensure they receive payment if the car is sold or damaged in an accident. The terms of car loan agreements vary depending on the lender's contract. In most cases, a car note that is more than 30 days is considered a breech of contract. Typically the lender notifies the borrower of the breech and any impeding plans to take possessions of the car, unless arrangements are made.

Many lenders hire contract firms to repossess automobiles. The contractors work on commission to repossess vehicles, which sometimes means that they disobey laws and grossly infringe on individuals rights such as attacking individuals, trespassing on personal property, and verbally accosting persons. See a knowledgeable attorney for more information.

OUT OF MONEY/SAVING MONEY

Don't feel alone if you've had to reach in your pocket to count change in order to purchase a hamburger or taco. Calling family late night to ask for money to pay utilities or rent is commonplace. Most of us have faced difficult times in our lives; finding help is available. Review some of the resources in the chapter in addition to those listed below and remember this too shall pass.

Location	Source
Books	Loos, Barbara. *I haven't Saved a Dime, Now What?* Silver Lining Books, © 2001.

Location	Source	
Web	www.livingfrugal.com www.miserlymoms.com www.handsnet.org http://anfdata.urban.org/incalc2 www.acf.dhhs.gov/programs/liheap/start.htm www.cheapskatemonthly.com www.stretcher.com www.esmarts.com www.finaid.org/loans/forgiveness.phtml www.unclaimed.org	
Agencies	**National Association of Unclaimed Property Administration** P.O. Box 7156 Bismarck, ND 58507 **The U.S. Department of Health and Human Services** 200 Independence Avenue, S.W. Washington, D.C. 20201 (202) 619-0257 Toll Free: 1-877-696-6775	**(TANF) Temporary Assistance for Needy Families** Administered by State Agencies 310 L'Enfant Promenade, SW Washington, DC 20447

EXCESSIVE DEBT

Gaining control of finances before they get out of hand is the best prescription for avoiding debts. Understandably, this is easier said than done. Once finances are out of control, a step-by-step plan must be made to identify which debts are a must to pay and which can be negotiated. The following resources provide information on regaining financial control when debts are high.

Location	Source
Books	Gudran, Nickel Maria, Attorney at law. *Your Rights When You Owe Too Much.* Sphinx Publishing. © 2001. Looning, Deanne, Robin Leonard. *Money troubles: Legal Strategies To Cope With your Debts 7th Edition.* Nolo Press, © 2001. Jerrold, Mundis. *How to Get out of Debt Stay Out of Debt & Live Prosperously.* Bantam Books, © 1987.
Web	www.livingfrugal.com www.ivillage.com/money www.quicken.com

FINANCIAL BUDGETING

Record keepers, software programs, and financial courses are excellent vehicles for budgeting. The success of financial budgets is depended upon your commitment and diligence, which can be tested when funds are low. Continue to budget in tough financial times as it oftentimes leads to greater economic stability when funds return.

Location	Source	
Books	Judy Lawrence. *The Budget Kit by 3rd Edition.* Dearborn Trade, © 2001. Garner, Robert J., Robert B. Coplan, Martin Nissenbaum, Barbara J. Rausch And Charles L. Rutner. *Earnest & Young*	Seotina, John E. *Managing to be Wealthy: Putting Your Financial Plan and Planner to Work For You.* Dearborn Financial Publishing, © 2000. Jaffe, Charles A. *The*

Location	Source	
	Personal Financial Planning Guide: Special tax Edition. John Wiley & Sons, Inc., (© in Earnest & young) © 2002.	*Right Way to hire Financial Help* MIT Press, © 1998
	Kay, Ellie. *How to Save Money Every Day.* Bethany House, © 2001.	Baker, Joseph M. *Finding the Financial Planner That's Right For You!.* Alcus Publishing, © 2001.
Web	www.napfta.org www.womenplanning.com www.armchairmillionaire.com www.quicken.com	www.cpf-board.org www.aicpa.org www.fpanet.org
Agencies	**National Association of Personal Financial Advisors** 355 W. Dundee Road Suite200 Buffalo Grove, IL 60089 (888) FEE- ONLY **American Institute of Certified Public Accountants** **Harbor side Financial Center** 201 Plaza Three Jersey City, NJ 07311-3881 (888) 999-9256 **Certified Financial Planner Board of Standards** 1700 Broadway Suite 2100 Denver, CO 80290-2101 (888) CFP-MARK	**American Institute of Certified Public Accountants Harbor Side Financial Center** 201 Plaza Three Jersey City, NJ 07311-3881 (888) 999-9256 **Financial Planning Association National Association of Personal Financial Advisors** 355 W. Dundee Road Buffalo Grove, IL 60089 (888) FEE-ONLY

DIFFICULTY PAYING UTILITIES

When economic currents turn for the worse, a significant expense is utilities. Utility companies have programs available for those who have little are no income. Inquire directly with local utility companies about programs available in addition to consulting the resources below.

Location	Source
Web	www.trac.org www.acf.dhhs.gov/programs/liheap/start.htm
Agencies	**Telecommunications Research and Action Center** (TRAC) Determining the best Phone Rates P.O. Box 27279 Washington, DC 20005 **Public Service Commission** (800) 342-3552

Chapter 10

Married, Unmarried, Separated, and Divorced

*To be happy at home is the ultimate result of
all ambition.*

Samuel Jackson

A ll of life experiences are based on relationships and it does not matter if you are married or single, developing healthy relationships begins with understanding oneself.

☼How The Information Was Found

Research was conducted by interviewing married and divorced persons in addition to web research. Persons interested in more books can visit self-help shelves in bookstores. My estimate is 85% of the books on the self-help shelves are relationship based.

Every month an excellent book with an interesting viewpoint on relationships hits the bookstands, which makes for a well documented topic.

I read the following inspirational article in a local newspaper. It addresses the experience of relationships - I hope that you will enjoy it as much as I do.

People come into your life for a reason, a season, or a lifetime. When you figure out which it is, you known exactly what to do. When someone is in you life for a REASON, it is usually to meet a need you have expressed outwardly or inwardly; they have come to assist you through a difficulty, to provide you with guidance and support, to aid you physically, emotionally, or spiritually.

They may seem like a Godsend, and they are; they are there for the reason you need them to be. Then without any wrong doing on your part or at an inconvenient time, this person will say or do something to bring the relationship to an end. Sometimes they die. Sometimes they walk away. Sometimes they act up or out and force you to take a stand. What we must realize is that our need has been met, our desire fulfilled; their work is done. The prayer you sent up has been answered and it is now time to move on.

When people come into you life for a SEASON, it is because your turn has come to share, grow, or learn; they may bring you an experience of peace or make you laugh; they may teach you something you have never done; they usually give you an unbelievable amount of joy. Believe it! It is real! But, only for a season.

LIFETIME relationships teach you lifetime lessons; those things you must build upon in order to have a solid emotional foundation. Your job is to accept the lesson, love the person/people (anyway); and put what you have learned to use in all other relationships and areas of your life. It is said that love is blind but friendship is clairvoyant.

Thank your lifetime relationships for being a part of your life...Smile and stop here if you're not into the final part: This is how you can show people you love them and to see how people love you!
Author Unknown

MARRIED

Committing to marriage is a huge responsibility. Taking on the emotional care and well beginning of another is a responsibility that millions of people have successfully accomplished. Knowing more about oneself including present and future expectations is essential to navigating through life with a partner who supports and shares similar objectives.

Location	Source
Books	Krasnow, Iris. *Surrendering to Marriage.* Miramax, © 2002. Love, Patricia. *The Truth About Love.* Fireside, © 2001. Harley, Willard F. Jr. *Fall in Love, Stay In Love.* Fleming H. Revell Co., © 2001.
Web	www.aamft.org www.smartmarriages.com http://1st-spot.net/topic_marriage.html
Agencies	**American Association for Marriage and Family Therapy** 112 South Alfred Street Alexandria, VA 22314-3061 (703) 838-9809 **Coalition For Marriage Family and Couples Education** 5310 Belt Road, NW Washington, DC 20015-1961

UNMARRIED/SINGLE

The choice not to marry is becoming increasingly popular. According to the results from the 2000 census, many Americans are choosing not to marry. Several factors contribute to this result. Certainly happiness is not found when one meets a spouse, it is found within. Being unmarried has its merits, joys and responsibilities. In researching this topic it was difficult to locate a central nationwide singles organization. Inquire from the web resources for local activities.

Location	Source	
Books	Amador, Xavier F., Judith Kiersky. *Being Single in a Couples' World: How to Be Happily Single While Looking for Love* Fireside © 1999. Anderson, Carol M. *Flying Solo: Single Women in Midlife*, W.W. Norton & Company ©1995.	Findling, Rhonda. *Don't Call That Man!: A Survival Guide to Letting Go.* Hyperion © 1999.
Web	www.singleactivities.com www.atlantasinglegourmet.com	

Finding a Partner

So you're ready to marry? Finding the person who is meant solely for you is the hope of all persons desiring marriage or long-term partnerships. Some people exhaust themselves searching for the perfect mate; they spend thousands of dollars on search firms and personal ads hoping to meet the person that is right for them. Many people are eagerly waiting for Mr. or Ms. right to cross their paths.

Location	Source	
Books	Huff, Carol, Wess Huff. *Perfect Partners* Empowerment Solutions, Inc © 1998. Mater, Rick. *Date to Win: How to Have More Dates, Find That Lasting Relationship, or Meet Your Ideal Marriage Partner.* Laurel Canyon Pr © 1995.	Ridgway, Peggi. *Romancing in the Personal Ads: How to Find Your Partner in the Classifieds.* Wordpictures ©1996.
Web	www.lovecity.com www.datingclub.com www.datingsiteguide.com	

SEPARATED

Separating could be the first step toward rebuilding a long lasting relationship with your partner, or it can be the time needed to see a better path for your life without your current partner. Legal separation occurs when one partner physically separates from the marriage, the laws are clear about when a separation occurs, especially if one person moves out of a common dwelling place. The following

resources are for those who want to learn more about
separating.

Location	Source
Books	Jones, Ann, Susan Schechter. *When Love Goes wrong.* Harper Collins, © 1992. Wanderer, Zev, Tracy Cabot. *Letting Go: A 12-Week Personal Action Program to Overcome a Broken Heart.* Dell Books ©1987. Chapman, Gary D. *Hope for the Separated: Wounded Marriages Can Be Healed.* Moody Press © 1996. Bodmer, Judy. *When Love Dies How To Save A Hopeless Marriage.* Word Publishing ©1999.
Web	www.aamft.org http://1st-spot.net/topic_marriage.html
Agencies	**American Association for Marriage and Family Therapy** 1133 15th street, NW, Suite 300 Washington, DC 20005 (202) 542-0109

DIVORCE

The collection of resources provide nationwide sources ready
to help those who are divorcing. The web sites have
information for person undergoing a range of divorces from
simple to complicated. One resource listed below,
www.divorcelawinfo.com, helps people locate family law
attorneys in any state.

Location	Source	
Books	Friedman, James T. *The Divorce Handbook.* Random House. © 1984. Paula James *The Divorce Mediation Handbook: Everything You Need to Know.* Jossey-Bass 1997.	Ahrons, Constance. *The Good Divorce.* HarperCollins © 1995.
Web	www.divorcelawinfo.com www.divorcenet.com www.divorceonline.com www.divorcedfather.com www.betterdivorce.com www.divorcesource.com www.divorcecare.com www.divorcesupport.com www.divorceinfo.com www.acfc.org	
Agencies	**National Long Distance Relationship Building Institute** 148 West 4750 North, Provo, UT 84604 (801) 224-4494 **MotherLinC. (MOMs Living Apart from their Children)** (850) 536-0139 (972) 274-2591 P.O. Box 1393, Dover, NH 03821-1393	**American Association for Fathers and Children** 1718 Main Street, NW Suite 187 Washington, DC 20036 (800) 978-DADS (3237) **American Coalition for Fathers and Children** 1718 M Street, NW, Suite 187 Washington, DC 20036 (800) 978-DADS

Child Custody and Visitation

Children are the innocent victims of divorce. Surprisingly, many children are comfortable with parents divorcing when it's thoroughly discussed. The courts attempt to ensure children are cared for emotionally and financially when one parent leaves. To learn more about custodial and non-custodial rights, see the resources below.

Location	Sources	
Books	Watnik, Webster. *Child Custody Made Simple.* Single Parent Press© 2000. Jasper, Margaret C. *The Law of Child Custody.* Oceana Publications © 1997. Boland, Mary L. *Your right to Child Custody, Visitation and Support.* Sphinx Publishing, © 2001.	*The Mother's Child Custody.* Handbook (2002 Edition) Divorce Source, © 2002. *The Father's Child Custody.* Handbook (2002 Edition) Divorce Source, © 2002.
Web	www.fatherhood.org www.menstuff.org www.ancpr.org www.childsupport-aces.org www.supportkids.com www.custodysource.com www.acfc.org www.fathersrc.com www.deadbeatparent.com www.divorcenet.com www.singlefathers.org	
Agencies	**American Father Coalition** 2000 Pennsylvania	**National Association for Child Enforcement of Support (ACES)**

Location	Sources
	Ave., NW, Suite 148 Washington, DC 20006	444 North Capitol Street, Suite 414 Washington, DC 20001-1512 (202) 624-8180

National Child Support Enforcement Association
444 North Capitol Street, Suite 414 Washington, DC 20001-1512 (202) 624-8180

Mothers Without Custody
P.O. Box 36 Woodstock, IL 60098

Alliance for Non Custodial Parental Rights
9903 Santa Monica Blvd., #267 Beverly Hills, CA 90212

Association Children Enforcement Support
2260 Upton Ave. Toledo, OH 43606 (800) 537-7072

Attorneys, Paralegals, and Self-Representation

The law isn't justice. It's a very imperfect mechanism. If you press exactly the right buttons and are also lucky, justice may show up in the answer. A mechanism is all the law was ever intended to be.

Raymond Chandler

Having the assistance of a legal expert is assuring to those who have, at some point, had questions navigating through the laws and regulations that govern our lives. Locating competent legal counsel and representation is like finding a gold mine. Clients must be involved with their case and be cooperative, while many others will take comfort in representing themselves.

☼How The Information Was Found

Finding a diligent and knowledgeable attorney is difficult. I can certainly advise which attorney's I would never hire to represent me again, but finding the right one takes meeting the acquaintance of those who didn't work out. The best hint for identifying an attorney is to find one who is responsive and has support staff to assist when his/her caseload become overwhelming. Complaints clients have of attorneys is their lack of response.

The information in this chapter was found by researching books and webs. The law library is a gold mine of information and, with the help of the law librarian; research is made easy.

The legal field is one of the fastest growing occupation in the United States; with so many attorneys, paralegals, legal secretaries, judges, law clerks, probation officers, and the host of others, understanding their roles is the first step to locating appropriate help. While you may find that representing yourself can easily and economically solve your legal troubles.

WHAT IS AN ATTORNEY

An attorney provides legal representation to those parties who have retained their services. Attorneys are certified or licensed (depending on the state) by a governing body, commonly known as the bar association for the state. Attorneys must be certified or licensed in order to practice law on another's behalf.

Types of Attorneys

Lawyers are like rhinoceroses: thick skinned, short-sighted, and always ready to charge.
David Mellor

Lawyers can specialize in a wide variety of areas. Probate (will, estates, trusts, etc.) criminal, family, personal injury (accidents), business, patent, employment, and labor to name a few. Law school students are introduced to a wide variety of legal subjects. However, most choose to specialize in at least two legal fields. An Attorney with too many specialties may prove disastrous for clients seeking competent personalized attention.

Selecting an Attorney

An attorney should posses both knowledge and drive. A *bad* attorney doesn't care and probably doesn't know how to help you. With so many attorneys' one is bound to come across one or more of the bad ones rather than the hard working concerned professionals. Before meeting with an attorney prepare a detailed outline of the events as they transpired, including the dates. Speak with the attorney over the telephone and fax the outline to his/her office, the outline helps you remember all the events in sequence and helps the attorney understand the issues of your case.

Location	Source
Books	Founberg, Jay G. *Finding the Right Partner.* American Bar Association, © 1995. Naifeh, Steven and Gregory White. *The Best Lawyers In America.* Woodward/white, Inc., © 2000.
Web	www.lawguru.com www.wld.com www.martindale.com www.uslaw.com
Agencies	**American Bar Association** 750 15th Street, NW Washington, DC 2005-1022 (202) 662-8690 **National Bar Association** 1225 11th Street, NW Washington, DC 20001 (202) 842-3900

Legal Representation for the poor or low-income

If one really wishes to know how justice is administered in a country, one does not question the policemen, the lawyers, the judges, or the protected members of the middle class. One goes to the unprotected-those, precisely, who need the law's protection most- and listen to their testimony.

James Baldwin

Depending on the nature of the case locating an attorney can be easy or challenging. Persons who have clear cut cases where the attorney is expecting to receive a portion of the monetary award he/she will be more likely to take the case with little regard to the persons ability to pay; the attorney receives a percentage of the settlement or award up to one-third. Attorneys also take pro bono (free of charge) cases on a client-by-client

Low-income persons and seniors may consider contacting local law schools for free or no cost legal assistance.

basis. Many attorneys provide their services free of charge within the community to make themselves accessible to those with little or no income. In addition, there are legal aid centers, often located near court buildings, with staff attorneys who provide assistance to the poor. Interested persons should contact the desired attorney's office to inquire about the policies for accepting low-income clients. Persons with little or no income may find justice by representing themselves, for more information see the self-representation section in this chapter.

Location	Source
Web	www.lsc.gov
	www.nlada.org
	www.consumerlaw.org
	www.povertylaw.org

Location	Source
	www.nationalbar.org www.clasp.org/NLADA/Civil/Civil_EJN www.ajs.prose/links.html www.povertylaw.org
Agencies	**National Consumer Law Center (NCLC)** 18 Tremont Street Boston, MA 12108 (617) 523-7398 **National Bar Association** 1225 11th Street, NW Washington, DC 20001 (202) 842-3900 **National Center On Poverty Law, Inc.** 205 West Monroe Street Chicago, IL 60606 (312) 263-3830 **National Legal Aid & Defender Associatio**n 1625 K Street NW, Suite 800 Washington, DC 2006-1604 (202) 452-0620	**LSC (Legal Services Corporation) Public Affairs** 750 1st Street, NE.10th Floor Washington, DC 2002 (202) 336-8800 (800) 688-9889- to locate the nearest office to you. **National Legal Aid and Defender Association** 1625 K. Street, NW.8th Floor Washington, DC 20006 (202) 452-0620 **American Bar Association** 750 15th Street, NW Washington, DC 2005-1022 (202) 662-8690 **The National Center on Poverty** 111 N. Wabash Ave., Suite 500 Chicago, IL, 60602

Firing an Attorney

Clients have the option of firing an attorney with or without reason. It's wise to dismiss an attorney in writing as well as verbally. Clients have a right to the originals of your file once you have terminated their services and made a written request. The attorney ensures that you have the current charges to date, in writing.

Filing a Complaint Against an Attorney

Problems between attorneys and clients are common. With the many lawyer jokes circulating it is amazing that attorneys remain employed. Some clients choose not to sue, but rather file a complaint against the attorney. State bar associations or licensing agencies process hundreds of complaints annually against attorneys. For more information on how to file a complaint refer to the resources below.

Location	Source
Books	Ostberg, Kay, and Theresa Meehan. *If You Want To Sue Your Lawyer: A Directory Of Legal Malpractice Attorneys.* Halt, © 1995. Starnes, Tanya, Attorney. *Mad At Your Lawyer: What To Do when You're Overcharged, Ignored Betrayed Or A Victim Of Malpractice.* Nolo Press, © 1996.
Web	www.abanet.org www.martindale.com
Agencies	**American Bar Association** 750 15th Street, NW Washington, DC 2005-1022 (202) 662-8690

What is a Paralegal

Paralegals have worked for attorneys and/or taken undergraduate classes for paralegal studies. Paralegals have a understanding of the law and depending on their experience, provide valuable insight on legal procedures; they are familiar with laws and can provide legal preparation services, however they cannot represent clients in or out of court. Persons choosing to represent themselves may find a knowledgeable paralegal that assists with the preparation of documents and provides assistance with determining the best course of action.

SELF-REPRESENTATION (PRO SE)

Citizens can stand before a judge without the assistance of an attorney. In some cases it can be beneficial not to have an attorney present, as it tends to incite additional problems, this is especially true of common divorces. With hundreds of useful self-help books on legal research and self-representation, representing yourself is no longer complicated and intimidating.

Retain the assistance of an attorney or paralegal to assist you with navigating through the legal system should you need additional coaching. You'll do the research and he/she can provide pointers or give direction. The fees for the consultations should be less expensive than retaining their services.

Location	Source
Books	Bergman, Paul and Sara J. Berman-Barrett. *Represent Yourself in Court.* Nolo Press © 1997.

Location	Source
	Battle, Carl W. *Legal-Wise*. Allworth Press, © 1991. Nelson, Jeffery A. *Sue The Bastard*. Contemporary Books, © 1999. Maier, Elaine C. *How To Prepare Legal Citation*. Barron's Educational Series, © 1986. Kramon, James M., Esq. *You Don't Need a Lawyer*. © 2002.
Web	www.halt.org www.ajs.prose/links.html www.nolo.com
Agencies	**HALT** (An Organization of Americans for Legal Reform) 1612 K. Street, NW Suite 510 Washington, DC 20006 (888) 367-4258

Legal Research

Legal research is made easy by using the Internet. With many states, colleges, and courts posting their entire codes and forms online obtaining the information you need is a click away. In addition, there are excellent books for understanding the ins and outs to legal research. Many cities and towns have law libraries located in or near superior court buildings, which are available for public use free of charge. Most college law libraries allow members of the public to visit, although most do not allow non-students to check out books. I found many resources for this book at the law library.

Location	Source
Books	Elias, Stephen Attorney and Susan Levin Kind. *Legal Research.* Nolo Press 7th Edition, © 1999. Larsenand, Sonja and John Bourdeau. *Legal Research For Beginners.* Barron's, © 1997.
Web	www.lawcornell.edu www.lexis.com www.westlaw.com www.nolo.com
Agencies	**LexisNexis Group (data gathering software company for laws)** P.O. Box 933 Dayton, Ohio 45401-0933 (937) 865-6800 (800) 227-9597

Legal Malpractice

Similar to medical malpractice, clients can sue attorneys for malpractice and recover damages. As with all types of disputes it's important to maintain detailed records to show a pattern of negligence or errors. Clients also have the option to file complaints with the state bar association. The complaint letters should be detailed and outline why and when the negligent behavior, see *filing a complaint against an attorney within this chapter.*

Chapter 12

Victims, Criminals, and Accused

*There is no despair so absolute as that which
comes with the first moments of our first great
sorrow, when we have not yet known what it
is to have suffered and be healed, to have
despaired and have recovered hope.*

George Eliot

F rom victims and criminals we can clearly see where we,
as a society, fail our members and identify issues that
are desperate for attention.

☼How The Information Was Found

The victims resources provided in this chapter are for violent crimes. *White Collar* crimes are included in Chapter 8 *Consumer Advocacy.* Families of murdered victims can find resources in Chapter 15 *Death & Dying.* Resources for child victims are included in this chapter as well as Chapter 2 *Parenting.*

Resources were located primarily via the Internet and by reading newspapers, magazines, books, etc. Victims of specific types of crimes can easily find information online, for example several rape victims have comforting web sites for other victims to share their experience.

Surprisingly, prison resources were numerous. Prison newsletters and papers can be easily found at alternative bookstores, although they were not included in this guide due to time constraints. The papers offer information on legislations for prison reforms in addition to other informative topics. Families affected by a loved ones incarceration can also find information from the resources provided in this chapter.

VICTIMS OF CRIMES

The following resources have been collected to address a variety of victim assistance programs. Additional information is found within the next few sections for topics such as domestic violence and crimes against children. In addition, there is a section for murders and suicide in Chapter 15 Death & Dying. The resources were designed to give information and comfort to those who find themselves victims of heinous crimes.

Location	Sources	
Web	www.elderabusecenter.org www.wetip.com www.try-nova.org	
Agencies	**National Center On Elder Abuse** 1225 1 Street, NW, Suite725 Washington, DC 20005 (202) 898-2586 **National Organization For Victim Assistance (NOVA)** 1757 Park Road, NW Washington, DC 20010 (202) 232-6682 **Rape, Abuse, and Incest National Network (RAIN)** (800) 656-4673 (800) 656-HOPE **National Center for Victims of Crime** 2000 M Street, NW #480	**Victims of Crime Resource Center** P.O. Box 6000 Rockville, MD 20850 (800) 627-6872 **We Tip Crime Hotline** P.O. Box 1296 Rancho Cucamonga, CA 91729-1296 (800) 782-7463 (800) 782-CRIME (800) 47-ARSON (800) 87-FRAUD (800) 47-DRUGS **National Victim Center** (703) 276-2880 (800) FYI-CALL

Location	Sources	
	Washington, DC 20036 (800) FYI CALL	**National Domestic Violence Hotline** (800) 799-SAFE (7233)

DOMESTIC VIOLENCE

Men, women and children are affected by domestic violence. The following resources provide support and assistance to victims of domestic violence.

Location	Sources	
Books	Evans, Patricia. *The Verbally Abusive Relationship.* Adams Media Corporation © 1996. Mariani, Cliff. *Domestic Violence Survival Guide.* Looseleaf Law Pubns Corp © 1996.	Berry, Bradley Dawn. *The Domestic Violence Sourcebook.* McGraw-Hill/Contemporary Books © 2000.
Web	www.besafe.org www.famvi.com www.best.com www.frpf.com	www.drsheltertour.org www.nnedr.org www.ncadv.org www.lambda.org
Agencies	**National Coalition Against Domestic Violence** P.O. Box 18749 Denver, CO 80218 (303) 839-1852 **LAMBDA** (gay and	**National Network to End Domestic Violence** 660 Pennsylvania Avenue, SE Suite 303 Washington, D.C. 20003

Location	Sources
lesbian antiviolence) PO Box 31321, El Paso, TX 79931-0321	(202) 543-5566

National Domestic Violence Hotline
(800) 799-SAFE (7223)
(800) 787-3224 (TDD)

Battered Women's Justice Project
c/o National Clearinghouse For The Defense Of Battered Women
125 South 9th Street, Suite 302
Philadelphia, PA 19107
(800) 903-0111 Ext.3
(215) 351-0010

National Clearinghouse for the Defense of Battered Women
125 South 9th Street, Suite 302
Philadelphia, PA 19107
(215) 351-0010

Center for the Prevention of Sexual and Domestic Violence 936 North 34th Street, Suite 200
Seattle, WA 98103
(206) 634-1903

Rape, Abuse, and Incest National Network (RAINN)
(800) 656-4673
(800) 656-HOPE

CRIMES AGAINST MINORS

Resources for crimes against minors are provided throughout this guide as a comfort to the innocent defenseless victims of our society (*also refer to Chapter 2 for additional resources*). Knowing that so many resources exist that serves the needs of children who have suffered some form of abuse is comforting and disconcerting. Parents must continually protect their children from harm, and if harm does occur immediately seek help.

Location	Sources	
Web	www.besafe.org www.foryourhealing.com www.missingkids.org http://ihave.org/	www.bbv.org www.cwla.org www.bowystown.org www.child.net
Agencies	**Bethel Bible Village** P.O. Box 729 Hixson, TN 37343 (423) 842-5757 **Child Welfare League of America** 440 First Street, NW Washington, CA 20001 (202) 942-0270 **Girls and Boys Town** 14100 Crawford Street Boys Town, NE 68010 (402) 498-1072 (800) 448-3000 national hotline **National Clearing House / Child Abuse** 330 C Street, SW Washington, DC 20447 (800) 394-3366 / (800) FYI-3366 **Mothers Against Sexual Abuse (MASA)** 503 1/2 S. Myrtle Ave. Suite 9 Monrovia, CA 91016 (626) 305-5190 **National Center for**	**Child Help USA** National Headquarters 15757 N. 78th St. Scottsdale, AZ 85260 (800) 422-4453 (24hrs) (800) 2-A-CHILD **Child Find America** 243 Main Street P.O. Box 277 New Pahz, NY 12561 (800) 426-5678 / (800) – I AM LOST **For Kids Sake** 24710 Washington Street, Suite 5 Murrieta, CA 92562 (800) 898-4543 **Incest Survivors Anonymous** P.O. BOX 17245 Long Beach, CA 90807-7245 (562) 428-5599 **Missing Children Help Center** 410 Ware Blvd. Suite 710 Tampa, FL 35617-4457 (800) 872-5437(24 Hr)

Location	Sources	
	Missing and Exploited Children (Also serves As The National Child Porn Tip Line) (800) 843-5678 (800) 826-7657 (TDD)	(800) USA-KIDS **National Children's Coalition (NCC)** 699 Prince Street Alexandria, VA 22314 (800) 843-5678
	Monarch Resources P.O. Box 1293 Torrance, CA 90505-0293 (310) 373-1958	**Find The Children** 1811 W. Olympic Blvd. Suite 107 Los Angeles, CA 90064 (310) 477-6721

HATE CRIMES

Crimes against underrepresented members of our society are commonly referred to as hate crimes; this topic also includes crimes against gay and lesbian persons. Locating nationwide resources was difficult as there isn't an abundance of agencies that serve the entire nation, however, there are many anti-hate centers located throughout the nation that serve their local communities. Persons who are a victim of a hate crime should consider the following resources as a beginning step to locating centers within your community.

Location	Source
Web	www.learnart.com
	www.xq.com
	www.glnh.org
	www.lambda.org
	www.aclu.org
	www.antiracist.com
	www.stopthehate.net
	www.tolerance.org
	www.stopthehate.org

Location	Source
	www.citizensagainsthate.com www.tagv.org

Location	Source	
Agencies	**Youth Action for Peace International Secretariat** 3, Avenue du Parc Royal 1020 Bruxelles Belgium +32 2 478 94 10	**Teens Against Gang Violence** 2 Moody St. Dorchester, MA 02124 (617) 282-9659
	The Gay and Lesbian National Hotline (888) THE-GLNH	**Canadian Anti-racism Education and Research Society** POB 2783 Vancouver, British Columbia Canada V6A 2E2 (604) 687.7350
	LAMBDA (gay and lesbian antiviolence) PO Box 31321, El Paso, TX 79931-0321	
	The Interfaith Alliance 1331 H St., NW 11th Floor Washington, D.C. 20005 (202) 639-6370	

APPREHENSION

Incarceration/Imprisonment (Prisoners and Families)

Programs are available to persons incarcerated and their families, particularly children. Most programs are religious organizations, however, there are a few that are not religion based. The following are a sample of the many resources that provide support to individuals, families, and children.

🔆 Families Against Mandatory Minimums (FAMM)
1612 K Street, NW, Suite 1400
Washington, DC 20006
(202) 822-6700
www.famm.org

Location	Sources
Book	Bergman, Paul and Sarah J. Berman-Barrett. (Attorney's). *The Criminal Law Handbook: Known Your Rights.* Nolo Press, © 1999.
Web	www.angletree.org www.e-ccip.org www.curenational.org www.fcnetwork.org www.fatherhood.org www.keepthetrust.org www.prisonsucks.com www.humanwrites.org www.openinc.org www.prisonactivits.org www.theprisonconnection.com www.prisonervisitation.org www.prisonlife.com www.spr.org
Agencies	**Center for Children of Incarcerated Parents** **Family and Corrections Network** 32 Oak Grove Road

Location	Sources
P.O. Box 41-286 Eagle Rock, CA 90041 (626) 449-8789 **CURE** P.O. Box 2310 Washington, DC 20013 (202) 789-2126 **Fathers Behind Bars** 525 Superior Street Niles, MI 49120 (616) 684-5715 fathersbehindbars2@ msn.com	Palmyra, VA 22963 (804) 589-3036 **Long Distance Dads** 101 Lake Forest Boulevard, Suite 360 Gaithersburg, MD 20877 (301) 948-0599 **National Incarcerated Muslim Network** 59 Darrington Road Rosharon, TX 77583 **National Trust for the Development of African- American Men** 6811 Kenilworth Avenue, Suite 501 Riverdale, MD 20737 (301) 887-0100

JUVENILE OFFENDERS (INCLUDING PROGRAMS FOR TROUBLED YOUTH)

A child's life going awry is a clear signal to parents that immediate attention is necessary to correct and address the issue(s). Oftentimes, one parent runs the household or two full-time working parents who do all they can to provide the basic needs for survival. Children are constantly being neglected and one form of showing their dissatisfaction is misbehaving and depending on the degree of neglect (and abuse) the misbehaving can quickly turn into major problems. The following resources may also be of service to parents as well as youths assisting with juvenile offenders and troubled youth. For more resources on troubled youth (and parenting), *see Problems At Home* in *Chapter 2.*

Location	Source	
Book	Bergman, Paul and Sarah J. Berman-Barrett. (Attorney's). *The Criminal Law Handbook: Known Your Rights.* Nolo Press, © 1999.	
Web	www.ncjj.org www.usdoj.gov/kidspage/ www.abanet.org/crimjust/jurjus www.ncjrs.org www.safeyouth.org http://ojjdp.ncjrs.org	www.ycwa.org www.abanet.org/child www.youthlaw.org www.jle.org www.cjcj.org www.boystown.org
Agencies	**Girls and Boys Town** 14100 Crawford Street Boys Town, NE 68010 (402) 498-1072 (800) 448-3000 national hotline	**Tough Love International** P.O. Box 1069 Doylestown, PA 18901 (800) 333-1069 www.toughlove.org

REBUILDING A LIFE AFTER INCARCERATION

Children have a lesson adults should learn, to not be ashamed of failing, but to get up and try again. Most of us adults are so afraid, so cautions, so "safe", and therefore so shrinking and rigid and afraid that is why so many humans fail.

El-Hajj Malik El-Shabazz
(Malcolm X)

Most people convicted of crimes are going to be free from their constraints at some point in time. The success of life outside of prison is determined by the resolve to grow and change while incarcerated. So many successful people throughout the world have been incarcerated; and many more are successful within their home by being an example to their family of how to change when given an opportunity.

Location	Sources	
Web sites	www.xoffenders.org	www.reentry.org
	www.ifiprison.org	www.4rw.org
	www.openinc.org	www.prisonactivist.org
	www.cellpals.com	www.nicic.org
	www.kairosprisonministry.org	
Agencies	**Kairos Outside** 140 North Orlando Avenue #180 Winter Park, FL 32789 (407) 629-4948 **Open, Inc. (Offender Preparation and Education Network, Inc.)** P.O. Box 472223 Garland, TX 75047-2223 (972) 271-1971 **Victory Outreach Ministries** 250 W. Arrow Hwy. San Dimas, CA 91770 **National Institute Of Corrections** 1860 Industrial Circle, Suite A Longmont, Colorado 80501 (800) 877-1461 (303) 682-0213 **Shoplifters Anonymous** (800) 848-9595 **Prison Activist Resource Center** P. O. Box 339	**Association of X-Offenders** 219 East Wm. Joel Bryan, TX 77803 (979) 775-9200 **Re-Entry Prison and Jail Ministry** P.O. Box 620 Chula vista, CA 91912 (619) 426-4557 **InterChange Freedom Initiative** 3807 G.H. South Peoria Tulsa, OK 74105 (914) 747-2932 **Human Rights Watch: Prisons** 350 Fifth Street, 34th Floor New York, NY 10118-3299 (212) 290-4700 **Federal Bureau of Prisons**

Location	Sources	
	Berkeley, CA 94701 (501) 893-4648	320 First Street, NW Washington, DC 20534 (202) 397-3198

RACIAL PROFILING & HARASSMENT

A couple of years ago the news media was focused on *racial profiling:* highlighting persons of color being harassed and physically beaten by police for no other reason but their color. As the brutality increased, outcries came from victims, families of victims and human rights organizations to put an end to the constant hostility directed to thousands, if not, millions of victims. As a result their efforts, the American Civil Liberties Union (ACLU) has filed a class action law suite on behalf of victims of racial profiling, and many individuals have pursued cases against local, county and state authorities seeking compensation for their damages. For more information consult the following resources:

Location	Source	
Web	www.aclu.org www.gjf.org www.minorityrights.org www.usccr.org	
Agencies	**Greensboro Justice Fund International**	**Minority Rights Group International (worldwide)**

Location	Source	
	P.O. Box 1594 Northampton, MA 01061 (413) 584-1079 (877) 585-6606	379 Brixton Road London, SW9 7DE, UK +44 (0)20 7978 9498
	American Civil Liberties Union (ACLU) 1400 20th St., NW, Suite 119 Washington, DC 20036 Tel.: (202) 457-0800 (Washington DC Office)	**National Bar Association** 1225 11th Street, NW Washington, DC 20001 (202) 842-3900
	United States Commission On Civil Rights U. S. Commission on Civil Rights 624 9th St., NW Washington, DC 20425 (800) 552-6843	**Community Relations Service** U.S. Department of Justice 5550 Friendship Blvd., Suite 300 Chevy Chase, MD 20815 (800) 347-4283

FALSE IMPRISONMENT/ FALSELY ACCUSED

With the millions of person incarcerated it is not surprising that some have been wrongfully imprisoned. Each *police scandal* reveals more victims of malicious policing and poor legal counsel. A few resources exist.

Location	Sources
Web	www.amnesty.org www.amnestyusa.org www.abuse-excuse.com/elusive_toc.htm

Location	Sources
Agencies	**Amnesty International** 322 8th Avenue New York, NY 10001 (212) 807-8400 **National Center for Victims of Crime** 2000 M Street, NW #480 Washington, DC 20036 (800) FYI CALL **Victims Of Child Abuse Legislation (VOCAL)** 11625 E. Old Spanish Trail Tuscan, AZ 85730-5615 (800) 743-8778

Location | Sources

Amnesty International
322 8th Avenue
New York, NY 10001
(212) 807-8400

**National Center for
Victims of Crime**
2000 M Street, NW
#480
Washington, DC
20036
(800) FYI CALL

Agencies

**Victims Of Child Abuse
Legislation (VOCAL)**
11625 E. Old Spanish
Trail
Tuscan, AZ 85730-5615

(800) 743-8778

Financial Planning and Understanding Financial Terms

*A man who both spends and saves money is
the happiest man, because he has both
enjoyments.*

Samuel Jackson

I once worked at a financial company that kept their employees well informed of financial planning strategies and hints for growing their current savings and retirement wealth. Even in that environment I couldn't learn all there is to know about managing finances. For those interested in financial planning, this chapter introduces helpful resources for all of the major investment sources along with a brief description of common financial terms. With some time and practice one can be equipped to fluently speak the financial lingo or at least understand what's being said.

✪How The Information Was Found

After reading the brief and simplified descriptions contained in this chapter along with researching the resources provided one could be on the road to understanding the scores of financial terms.

I purchased several books at a major bookstore chains that lead me to other books. I must caution that some books, not included, were a huge disappointment. If you're just beginning to read about investment you should not be disappointed in the selections listed under books, as it took many months to locate the proper text. I would suggest purchasing the [6]Finance & Investment Handbook by Barron's on investment terms as a companion to this chapter, a new edition cost around $35 but an older edition is suitable and costs less. For those who are seriously interested in investment, the Barron's book is a must have.

The web sites I located were great! Some sites provided a different angle on the same subject. It's worth your while to log onto two or more sites to gain an understanding of the topic. Similar to the other sections the resources were located by web, interviews, and book research.

---

[6] Downes, John, Jordan Elliot Goodman. *Finance & Investment Handbook* © 1999.

UNDERSTANDING INVESTMENTS

Understanding investment begins with understanding your financial goals. Persons who are not heavily involved in the investment circle often find themselves lost when discussions about finances arise, this should not be the case, although it is understandable. Investing is not as complicated as some may think, especially the type of investing most people engage with little to moderate wealth. After reading this chapter you should gain a solid understanding of financial terms. Depending on your objective there are different paths to investing; persons who have long term goals of accumulating substantial wealth for retirement, are wanting to increase their savings over the next few years, an/or a desire to get rich now. Some people find that they want to accomplish all three objectives or a combination of investing goals. Understanding your objective(s) helps with locating the type of plan that range from conservative, moderate to aggressive. For example, If you are 23 years old and plan to work until the have of 65 you have 42 years to accumulate wealth, which allows the person to invest in conservative plans that grows slowly and are not affected by volatile market shifts. Their investment portfolio could have 90% invested in bonds and 10% invested in stocks. Persons who are 36 years old and plan to retire at the age of 65 this person has 29 years to build their retirement nest. This person may want to choose a moderate plan that is includes conservative bonds and aggressive stocks. A retirement plan portfolio for them may include 50% bonds and 50% stocks. Someone reaching the ago of 47 and plans to retire at the age of 65 has 18 years to plan for their retirement. These persons should consider an aggressive portfolio with 80% stocks and 20% conservative bonds.

Many brokers and representatives have wonderful color charts along with research that supports their claims to show retirement investors.

Employers often contribute to a retirement or pension plan for their employees; these investment accounts often allow persons to rollover the savings to another account retirement account (including IRA's, discussed in the following sections) should you change employers.

Location	Source	
Books	Bonham, Bryan Howard, CFA. *The Complete Investment and Financial Dictionary,* Media *Corporation,* © 2001.	Williamson, Gordon k. *First Time Investor.* Adam Media Corp, © 2001.
	Downes, John, Jordan Elliot Goodman. *Finance & Investment Handbook* © 1999.	Robbins, Mike. *Smart Guide to Planning Retirement.* Cader book, © 1999.
Web	www.investors.com www.Investopedia.com www.ultexinvostore.com www.pbgc.gov www.financialweb.com www.edgar.com www.businesswek.com www.investorama.com www.directadvice.com www.investorsguide.com www.hoovers.com www.individualinvestors.com	www.smartmoney.com www.stocksense.com www.amex.com www.barrons.com www.bloomberg.com www.netrest.com www.moneyline.com www.gomez.com www.aaii.org www.investorama.com www.greenmoney.com

Location	Source
Agency	**American Association of Individual Investors** 626 N. Michigan Ave. Chicago, IL 60611 (800) 428-2244

MUTUAL FUNDS (TYPES OF EMPLOYER SPONSORED AND INDIVIDUAL RETIREMENT)

The strategies for retirement investing depend on the age you began saving and the amount you have put forward to retirement. The trend has turned from people retiring with little or no money to those who have millions in excess cash.

Location		
Books	Kazanjian, Kirk. *Mutual Fund Investor's Guide 2002* New York Institute of Finance, © 2002. Casey, Mark and Kevin King. *Mutual Fund 500 2000 Edition.* Morning Star, Inc., © 2000. Hall, Alvin D. *Getting Starting in Mutual Funds.* Wiley, John & Sons, Inc., © 2000.	
Web	http:// Personalfund.com www.fundlibary.com www.fundinteractive.com http:// fund alarm.com	www.morningstar.com www.mfeu.com www.imoneynet.com www.mfea.com www.tiaa-cref.com
Agencies	**Morning Star** (800) 735-0700 **TIAA-CREF** (800) 223-1200	

401(k) plans

Private industry employers offer 401(k) retirement plans, as they allow employees to contribute a percentage of their pre-tax income, thereby reducing their gross income (this is an advantage to those who are in a high tax bracket). Most employers contribute a percentage of funds, in addition to the employee's contribution, into the retirement fund (having worked at different companies, large and small, I have only known of one employer who refused to contribute to their employees retirement). The percentage contributed varies by company.

Location	Source	
Books	Scott, Gilpatric. *Investing in 401(k)* Plans. IDG Book World Wide, Inc., © 2000. Perrin, Tower. *The Hand Book of 401(k) Plan Management (Revised Edition).* Irwin Professional Publishing, © 1997. Rowland, Mary. *Common Sense Guide to Your 410(k).* Bloomberg Press, © 1997. Warren, Boroson. *Keys to investing in your 401(k) 2nd Edition.* Barron's Educational Series, Inc., © 2000.	Bogosian, Wayne G., Robert Clark, Dee Lee. *The Complete Idiots Guide to 401(k) Plans.* Pub. Alpha Books, © 1998. Salisbury, Dallas and Marc Robinson. *IRA and 401(k) Investing.* Dorling Kindersley Publishing, Inc., © 2000.
Web	www.fool.com www.financialengines.com http://401k.mpower.com www.mpowercafe.com	www.cliffnotes.com www.401kate.com http://401k.mfs.com

403(b) Plans

Non-profit and tax-exempt employers can offer the 403(b) retirement savings plan to staff. 403(b) is a custodial account in which vesting almost immediately occurs. Both the employee as well as the employer can contribute to employee's 403(b) retirement plans; they operate similarly to 401(k) plans in that deductions to the plan are pre taxed, and taxes are taken at the time of withdrawal.

Location	Source	
Books	Pam, Horowitz. *Winning With Your 403(b)*. John Wiley & Sons, Inc., © 2001. Lowdler, Eleanor A. *403(b) Plans*. Dearborn Trade, © 1999.	*Working With Tax Sheltered Annuities 403(b) Plans Explained*. CCH Incorporated, © 2001.
Web	www.retirementplan.com www.moneymanagement /403b.html www.timyounkin.com www.403b-tga-com www.sensible-investor.com/403.html	
Agencies	**Pension Rights Center** 1140 19th Street, NW Suite 602 Washington, DC 20036 (202) 296-3776	**Pension and Welfare Benefits Administration Department of labor** 200 Constitution Avenue, NW Room N 5625 Washington, DC 20210 (202) 219-8776 (800) 998-7542

Pension Plans

Employers contribute 100% to pension plans for employees. Pension plans are designed for employees who stay with companies for many years. Most government and state employees receive a pension plan.

Location	Source	
Books	Schloss, Irving S. and Deborah V. Abildsoe *Understanding TIAA-CREF.* Oxford University Press Inc., © 2000. West Publishing Company. *Employee Benefit Plan in a Nutshell 2nd Edition.* © 1998. Allen, Everett T., Jr., Joseph J. Melone, Jerry S. Rosenbloom. *Pension Planning: Pensions, Profit-Sharing, And Other Deferred Compensation Plans.* McGraw-Hill/Irwin © 1997.	Matthews, Joseph Attorney at Law with Dorothy Berman Matthews. *Social Security, Medicare & Government Pension.* Nolo, © 2002. John, Langbein H.H. and Bruce A. Wol. *Pension and Employees Benefit Law 3rd Edition.* Foundation Press, Inc., © 2000.
Web	www.quicken.com/retirement/planner www.pensionplace.com www.pensionplanners.com www.pbgc.gov	

Keogh Plans

Keogh retirement plan is especially designed for self-employed persons, partners who file Schedule E, and Schedule C (1099) contractors who desire to contribute tax-deferred moneys to a retirement account. Self-employed individuals are attracted to Keogh plans because of the maximum contribution is as high as $30,000 or 25%, whichever is less, of self-employment income compared to the $2,000 contribution cap for IRAs.

Location	Source	
Books	Twila, Slesmick & John C Suttle. *Creating Your Own Retirement Plan: A Guide to Keoghs & IRA's for the Self-Employed.* Nolo, © 2001. Bambi, Holzer. *Getting Yours.* Johnson Wiley & Sons, © 2002.	Fishman, Stephen. *Working For Yourself.* 3rd Edition. Nolo Press, © 2001. Sherman, Michael. *The Retirement Calculator: Complete Saving and Withdrawal Table for IRA and Keogh Plans.* NTC/Contemporary Publishing, © 1986.
Web	www.tiaa-cref.org/keogh www.ekeogh.com www.irainvestor.com/smallbusiness/keogh/index.asp www.planinfo.com/keogh.html	

IRA (Individual Retirement Account)

IRA is a tax-deferred personal retirement funds that can be either tax deductible or taxable. The yearly maximum contribution amount for IRAs is $2,000 for singles or married couples filing separately or $4,000 for married couples filing jointly. IRAs are tax deductible if neither spouse participates in a qualified [retirement] plan. Many financial institutions offer IRA plans to customers. To learn more about IRAs or to locating resources or obtaining an IRA refer to the resources:

Location	Source	
Books	Buchanan, Kirk D. *The IRA Explanation: A User's Guide to the Individual Retirement Account*. Buchanan Resources, © 1994. Goldberg, Seymour. J.K. *Lesser's How to Protect Your Retirement Saving from the IRS, 3rd Edition*. Macmillan General Referral, © 1999. Sherman, Michael. *The Retirement Calculator: Complete Saving and Withdrawal Table for IRA and Keogh Plans*. NTC/Contemporary Publishing, © 1986.	Salisbury, Dallas and Marc Robinson. *IRA and 401(k) Investing*. Dorling Kindersley Publishing, Inc., © 2000. Twila, Slesmick & John C. Suttle. *Creating Your Own Retirement Plan: A Guide to Keoghs & IRA's for the Self-Employed*. Nolo, © 2001. Slesnic, Twila and John C Suttle. *IRA'S, 401(Ks) and Other Retirement Plans*. Nolo Press, © 2002.
Web	www.quicken.com/cms/viewers/article/retirement/18288 www.simpleirasite.com www.ire.com www.4thebank.com/iratradhtml	

Roth

Roth IRAs allow persons whose adjusted gross income is less than [7]\$100,000 to pay an initial tax at the time of investing rather than waiting until retirement withdrawal (these persons must have had the Roth IRA for at least 5 years). The maximum yearly contribution is the same as with a traditional IRA, \$2,000 for singles and married couples filing separately or \$4,000 for married couples filing jointly.

Location	Source	
Books	Goldberg, Seymour. *J .K. Lesser's How to Protect Your Retirement Saving from the IRS, 3rd Edition.* Macmillan General Referral, © 1999. Bledsoe, John D. *Roth to Riches: The Ordinary to Roth IRA Handbook.* Legacy Press, Inc., © 1998.	Trock, Gary R. *The Roth IRA Made Simple*, Conquest Publishing, © 1998. Gobind, Daryanani, Ph.D. *Roth IRA Book: An Investor's Guide 2nd edition.* Digiqual Inc.
Web	www.roth-advisor.com www.fairmark.com/rothira www.datachimp.com www.rothira.com	

---

[7] Persons whose earned income is greater than \$100,000 can contribute to a Roth IRA, However the investment is taxes.

Salary Reduction (Sep) IRA

Sep IRAs are designed for sole proprietorships and business that employ less than 25 full-time workers. The following resources are available to those who want to know more about Seps:

Location	Source
Books	Lesser, Gary S., *Simple SEP and SARSEP Answer Book*. Aspen Publishing, © 1997.
Web	www.e-analytics.com www.sep-ira-plan.com www.quicken.com/cms/views/article/retirement/18367

Simple IRA

Simple IRAs are designed for sole proprietorships and business that employ less than 100 full-time workers. The following web resources are for persons who have a Simple IRA or want to know more information:

Location	Source
Books	Lesser, Gary S., *Simple SEP and SARSEP Answer Book*. Aspen Publishing, © 1997.
Web	www.simpleira-site.com www.mkbcpa.com/simpleira.htm www.raffa.com/interior/simpleira.html http://retireplan.about.com/library/blpub560htm

Annuities

Life insurance companies issue annuities. The insurance company pays investors the interest stated on the contract, usually at the time of retirement age. Two types of annuities are offered: fixed (paid on regular installments) variable (payout based on a guaranteed number of units). Banks and financial services companies typically sell annuities.

Location	Source	
Books	Lane, Michael F. *Guaranteed Income for Life.* McGraw Hill Professional Publishing, © 1998. Breuel, Brian H. *The Complete Idiots Guide to Buying Insurance and Annuities.* Alpha Books, © 1996	Williamson, Gordon K. *Getting Started in Annuities. John Wiley & Sons, © 1998.* Shapiro, David and Thomas F. Streiff. *Annuities.* Dearborn Trade, © 2001.
Web	www.annuityshopper.com www.annuitynet.com www.annuity.com www.navanet.org www.morningstar.com	
Agencies	**Web Annuties.com** 8 Talmadge Drive Monroe Twp, NJ. 08831 (800) 872-6684 **National Association for Variable Annuities** 11710 Plaza America Dr, Suite 100 Reston, VA 20191	**Annuity Net** 108-G South Street Leesburg, VA 20175 (877) 927-8328 or (877) 835-5820 **Teachers Insurance and Annuity** Association-College Retirement Equities Fund TIAA-CREF

Location	Source
	730 Third Avenue New York, NY 10017-3206 (800) 842-2776 (800) 842-2755 (TTY)

Savings

Most all banks offer savings accounts that provide relatively low yielding interest on deposits. Persons desiring to have ready access to cash deposits and do not have the amounts required to invest in a money market account, savings prove to be an excellent alternative to earning interest and avoiding withdrawal fees. Some banks offer discounts on other accounts if saving deposits exceed a set limit. Most savings accounts are offered free of monthly fees to customers.

Location	Source	
Books	Pollack, Kenan, and Erick Heigheger. *The Real Life Investing Guide*. McGraw-Hill Professional, © 1997. Tyson Eric, and David Silvermore. *Personal finance For Dummies*. Hungary Minds, Inc., © 2000. Priddy Patterson, Martha. *The New Working Woman's guide to Retirement Planning*, University Of Pennsylvania Press, © 1999.	Walker, David M. *Retirement Security*. John Wiley & Sons, Inc., © 1996. O'Neill, Barbara M. *Saving On A Shoestring*. Dearborn trade, © 1994.
	http://moneycentral.msn.com/smartbuy/home.asp	

Location	Source
Web	www.wfla.com
	www.finance.com
	www.mmintl.org
	www.financeter.com

CDs (certificate of deposit)

CDs are high yielding saving accounts that *locks in* the deposits for a specified period usually ranging from 6 months to 5 years. Because of the high yield banks charge a penalty fee, 10-15%, for early withdrawal. Most banks offer CD's to customers. It's important to check with several banks before investing money into a CD, as banks offer different rates, and if you are willing to part with your money for one year or more you can receive the greatest yield possible.

Location	Source
Books	Champlin, Jeffery H. *The Bank Customer's Guide to Safe and Smart Investing.* McGraw-Hill Companies, © 1995.
Web	www.bankrate.com
	www.banxquote.com
	www.imoneynet.com

Money Markets

Money market accounts are relatively high interest yielding (meaning more interest is paid on deposits to money market account than those on standard savings accounts) offered by banks. Persons can save more money while retaining immediate access to their cash without incurring penalties. Banks require minimum deposit ranging from $500 – $2,500. Different types of money market accounts are available; the differences are based on the amounts deposited.

Location	Source
Books	O'Shaughness, Lynn. *Investing Bible.* Hungary minds Inc., © 2001.
Web	www.bankrate.com www.411-money.com www.moneyrates.com

INVESTMENT CLUBS

Being a member of an investment club provides hands on learning experience with personal investment that can be to lucrative. Each member of the investment club participates in researching investment perspectives like stocks, bonds, and funds, which helps the club members to become knowledgeable of unfamiliar terminology. I've attended a few investment club meetings and I was very impressed. Even the least interested person has knowledge about how to invest his/her monies. My eldest sister began an investment club and now she sounds like a financial broker. Becoming a member of an investment club requires regular attendance to receive full benefits, most clubs meet once a month.

Location	Source
Books	O'Hara, Thomas E. & Kenneth S. Janke. Sr. *Strut and Running Profitable Investment Club.* Three Rivers Press, © 1998.

Location	Source
	Gerlach, Douglas and Angele McQuade. *Investment Clubs* Hungry minds, © 2002. Bertrand, Marsha. *Getting Starting Investment Club.* John Wiley & Sons, Inc., © 2001.
Web	www.investmentclub.about.com www.better-investing.org www.flagship.vanguard.com www.investorguide.com www.bivio.com www.hh-club.com
Agencies	**National Association of Investors Corporation** P.O. Box 220 Royal Oaks, MI 48068 (877) 275-2642

STOCKS

My grandmother enjoys traveling to Las Vegas to gamble. She has gone so often that she says that she own a brick at the hotel where she enjoys staying. One brick is not worth much. However, had she purchased the hotel's stock, by this time, it would be worth quite a bit. Stock allows buyers to own shares of a company. Stockowners, or what they're commonly referred to as shareholders, purchase shares made available by the corporation thereby becoming eligible to receive a percentage of return on a company's earning and assets, for as long as the shareholder owns the stock and the company remains in operation. Instead of buying a brick one purchases a certificate that states how much they own in a company.

Two types of shareholders exist common and preferred. A company can issue both types of stock or only one, and they can set the contractual obligations in accordance with the guidelines set forth by the Security and Exchange Commission (SEC). The benefit to owning common stock is that holders are traditionally afforded the right to vote in the election of directors and regarding other matters. Traditionally, preferred stock holders are not given voting privileges, however, dividends are paid first to preferred stockholders and they receive first claim on assets and earning, which is important if the company should fold.

Depending on the contractual terms set forth by the stock issuer, persons can hold onto stock for years, even leave it to their estate or a beneficiary, or they can sell it within seconds of purchasing like those who practice in day trading.

Location	Source
Books	Scott, David L. *How Stocks Work*. McGraw-Hill Inc., © 2002. Mladjenovic, Paul. *The Unofficial guide to Picking Stocks*. IDG Books Worldwide, Inc., © 2001. O'Neil, William J. *How to Make Money in Stocks 2nd Edition*. McGraw-Hill, Inc., © 1998. Carlson, Charles B. *Buying Stocks Without A Broker*. McGraw-Hill, Inc., © 1992.
Web	www.stocks.com http://library.thinkquest.com www.marketdigest.com www.bigcharts.com www.fool.com www.morningstar.com www.thestreet.com www.zacks.com

Stock Options

Stock options allow employees to purchase company stock at an *introduction* price, once they're vested (a set time employed at the company), typically the price is lower than current market rates. During the dot-com boom, companies offered an enormous amount of stock options for employees to offset pay. Many of the companies never obtained the capital worth for public trading; these employees have lost a tremendous amount of income and savings when the companies went out of business. As the company grows so does your stock option value.

BONDS

As stocks are to partial ownership in companies, bonds are to loans to companies. Bond issuers are obligated to repay the principal amount of bonds at the time of maturity plus any interests to be paid at specified intervals. Bond investors are not provided voting privileges as stockholders, as they are lenders to the company and not shareowners. Three main categories for bonds are: corporate, government, and municipals bonds. Each category is explained in the following sections. Bonds are rated on a scale by their possibility to default; bonds with AAA have little risks than those with D ratings, bonds already in default. The lower rating bonds are referred to as junk bonds; these bonds offer a high interest rate which equates to greater profits for bond investors, but there is also a greater risk that the company may default.

Corporate Bonds

Private corporations desiring to obtain funding often issue bonds that are repaid at a specified time in the future, usually the face value. Corporate bonds are traded through the open market on open exchanges. Corporate bonds are taxable.

Government Bonds

The US treasury issues treasury bonds, notes, and bills to help fund the US government. These bonds are the safest and most risk free bonds offered to investors. The US government backs these investments and has never defaulted. The interest paid on government bonds is based on the interest rate.

~ Treasury bonds interest paid in semiannual installments

~ Treasury notes interest paid in semiannual installments

~ Treasury bills, interest is deducted from purchasing price, sold at a discount

Savings Bonds

The US government offers savings bonds for purchase for half their face value. Two types of savings bonds are: EE bonds and HH bonds. EE bonds mature in 30 years, however they can be redeemed at anytime after 6 months from the purchase date. EE bonds are exempt from state and local taxes, until redeemed. HH bonds cannot be purchased they can only be obtained from the exchange of EE bonds; they have a fixed annual percentage rate.

Location	Source	
Books	Faerber, Esme. *Fundamental of the Bond market.* McGraw-	Cohen, Marilyn With Nick Watson. *The Bond Bible.* New York

Location	Source	
	Hill Companies Inc., © 2001.	Institute of Finance, © 2000.
	Zipt, Robert. *How The Bond Market Works.* New York Institute of Finance, © 1997.	Faerber, Esme. *All About Bonds and Bond Mutual Funds. 2nd Edition*, McGraw-Hill Inc., © 2000.
	Sheino, Michael. *Bond Market Rules.* McGraw-Hill, Inc., © 2000.	
Web	www.bonds-online.com www.investingbond.com www.investinginbonds.com www.bondsonline.com www.publicdebt.treas.gov www.convertbond.com	
Agencies	**Bureau of Public Debt** Parkersburg, WV 26106-2186 (800) 465-BOND/ (800) 487-2663 (304) 480-6112	**Treasury Direct** P.O. Box 9150 Minneapolis, MN 55480-9150 (800) 722-2678

Municipal Bonds

State and local municipalities/agencies issue municipal bonds for either public or private purposes. Those bonds issued for public purposes are exempt from state, city, and local taxes and are issued without limit. Private purpose municipal bonds are taxable. Municipal bonds are considered safe, similar to US government bonds, although the rating may be slightly lower.

Bonds offered outside of the US are referred to international bonds. International bonds are sold on the open market and subject to the currency exchanged but are otherwise similar US Bonds.

INVESTMENT BROKERS

Knowledgeable investment brokers are worth their commissions and some. For the public to trade stock they must use the services of a broker. Having someone who's accessible and available to meet your demands is valuable. Investment brokers are licensed by the state and should be bonded. Many brokers work at firms or they can operate small business in communities. As with any other professional service, it's wise to research the broker's background prior to commencing transactions. For fraudulent practices of investment brokers, *see Chapter 8 Consumer Advocacy.*

Location	Source
Web	www.nasd.com/it4ao1.html
	www.ndb.com
	www.charlesschwab.com
	www.keynote.com
	www.mldirect.com
	www.smartmoney.com
	www.cyberivest.com

INVESTORS RESOURCES

Several *informational* books and websites are available to assist investors with tips and information that could be otherwise unknown such as changes in the law or status of companies. Some books provide detailed information that investors must know before commencing transactions. In addition there are newspapers and magazines that provide investment tips for readers.

Location	Source	
Books	Jason, Julie. *J. K. Lasser's Strategic Investing After 50.* John Wiley & Sons. Inc., © 2001 O'Neill, Barbara. *Investing on a Shoe String.* Dearborn, © 1999. Rye, David E. *1,001 Ways to Save, Grow, and Invest Your Money. Career Press,* © *1999.*	
Web	www.cftc.gov www.investorguide.com www.investools.com www.analysiszone.com www.progressivefutures.com www.futuresview.com www.abovetrade.com www.bestcalls.com www.cyberinvest.com www.traderspain.com www.ipodata.com www.iposources.org	
Agencies	**The National Futures Association (NFA)** (800) 676-4NFA National Association of Securities Dealers, Inc. (NASD) (800) 289-999 **U.S. Commodity Futures Trading Commission (CFTC)** Office of Public Affairs	**Certified Financial Planner Board of Standers** 1700 Broadway Suite 2100 Denver, CO 80290 (888) CFP-MARK

Location	Source
	La Fayette Center 1155 21st Street, NW Washington, DC 20581 (202) 418-5080

ONLINE TRADING

A major Internet success is online trading, which attracts thousands of investors daily. Online trading is fast and provides real-time results. The requirements for investing online depend on the institution. Persons who are reluctant to establish an account online can speak with their investment broker who can setup an account in person or over the telephone.

Location	Source	
	Guide to Online Investing: Become a Successful Internet Investor. Dow Jones& Co., Inc., © 2000.	Gilbert, Jill, Thomas S. Gray and Claire Mencke.*line Investing Bible.* IDG Books Worldwide, Inc., © 2001.
	Carey, Theresa W. *Guide to Online Investing. K.I.S.S. (Keep It Simple Series) Guide to Online Investing.* D k Publishing, © 2001.	Sindall, Kathleen. *Investing Online for Dummies.3rd Edition.* IDG Books Worldwide, Inc., © 2000.
Books		
Web	www.hoovers.com www.greenmoney.com www.kiplinger.com www.quicken.com www.quote.com www.wallstreetcity.com	

BILL PAYING ONLINE

Paying bills online is convenient. Used in conjunction with programs that assist with money management, persons can easily establish a household budget and manage they finances effectively. Most banks offer online bill paying services.

Location	Source
	www.bankrate.com
	www.onlinebankingreports.com
	www.banksite.com
	www.paypal.com
Web	

Chapter 14

Senior Rights and Resources

*I am only one; but I am still one. I cannot do
everything, but still I can do something. I will
not refuse to do the something I can do.*
Helen Keller

G rowing older is a blessing that should not be
frowned upon, as we all, over time, get older.
One reaches the stage, if all goes well, where
one is no longer concerned about the reaction of
others. Children become adults who are busy living their
independent lives and now it's time to put to use the benefits
entitled to seniors. The topics in this section were carefully
selected to address the concerns new and existing seniors
may have.

☼How The Information Was Found

Resources for seniors weren't difficult to locate. Most of the information is straightforward and the web sites remained present over the three years it took to complete this guide. Seniors wanting more information can log onto the web sites and look for additional links and resources. Most of the web pages have links to organizations that offer assistance.

SENIOR CITIZENSHIP

A set time in an aging hasn't been established for becoming a senior citizen. The Association for Retired Persons (AARP) provides anyone 50 years old or over membership. The United States government doesn't have a set age for senior citizenship, however those over the age of 62 can apply for benefits such as social security, Medicare, and housing (if needed).

SUPPORT GROUPS AND ACTIVITIES

Senior citizenship does not imply that one is too old for engaging in social activities like their younger counterparts. Many seniors are fit, active, and energetic with more free time available, which is ideal for someone looking for challenging experiences or simply stitching a sweater. Most of the retirement communities have activities for seniors; many cities throughout the US have constructed senior citizen centers that offer nutrition, financial, health, travel, and training courses, to name a few.

Location	Source
Books	Silton, Peter. *Active Retirement for Affluent Workaholics* NP Financials, © 2001. West, Joe. *300 Incredible Things For Seniors On The Internet.* Paul Jaffe, Keen Leebow, © 2000.

Location	Source
Web	www.unitedseniorshealth.org www.aarp.org www.aoa.gov./eldercare www.generationsonline.com www.eldercraftsmen.org www.nationalservice.org www.nsga.com http://senior-site.com www.seniorsearch.com www.wiredseniors.com www.ederhostel.org www.grandtimes.com
Agencies	**Eldercare Locater** (800) 677-1116 Nationwide Directory Assistance Helping Older People and Caregivers **Elder Hostel** 11 Avenue De Lafayette Boston, MA 0211-1746 (877) 426-8056 (877) 425-2167 (TTY) **Elder Craftsmen** 610 Lexington Ave. New York, NY 10022 (212) 319-8128 **Corporation for National Service** 1201 New York Avenue, NW Washington, DC 20525 (800) 424-8867	**Support Groups for Senior** 409 Third Street, SW Ste. 200 Washington, DC 20024-3212 **AARP (American Association of** Retired Persons) 601 E Street, NW Washington, DC 20049 (202) 424-3410 **Generations Online** 108 Ralston House 3615 Chestnut Street Philadelphia, PA 19104 (215) 222-6400

Location	Source
	(800) 833-3722(TTY) **National Senior Games** **Association** P.O. Box 82059 Baton Rouge, LA 70884-2059 (225) 925-5678

LOBBIES FOR SENIORS

Seniors who are interested in political action or who want to find current information on bills that affect persons over the age 62 can contact several major lobbies and political action groups. In addition to the resources listed below, most state and federal elected officials provide assistance with locating regional political action groups.

Location	Source
Web	www.ncscrnc.org www.graypanthers.org www.aarp.org www.apeape.org
Agencies	**Gray Panthers** 733 15th Street, NW, Suite 437 Washington, DC 20005 (800) 280-5362 **AARP (American Association of Retired Persons)** 601 E Street, NW Washington, DC 20049 (202) 424-3410

Location	Source
	Association For Protection of The Elderly(APE) 528 A Columbia Ave. Suite 127 Lexington, SC 29072 1-800-569-7345

RECEIVING SENIOR BENEFITS

Around the age of 50 years old, one can begin receiving some form of benefit because of age, such as membership eligibility to senior organizations such as AARP. For US citizens, the Social Security Department distributes individual year-to-date contributions one has made towards retirement, which details the amount of benefits one is eligible for upon retirement. For working seniors it's important to receive information on your retirement plan contributions from an employer. The combined amount along with any other financial savings is your retirement wealth.

Location	Source
Web	www.benefitscheckup.org/ www.heritage.org/research/features/socialsecurity www.ssa.gov www.aarp.org
Agencies	**AARP (American Association of Retired Persons)** 601 E Street, NW Washington, DC 20049 (202) 424-3410 **Social Security Administration** Baltimore, MD 21235

Location	Source
	(410) 956-2736
	(800) 772-1213

RETIREMENT

One can retire at any age, but most wait until they have financial wealth or are able to receive payouts from retirement plans and/or savings. The US government pays citizens who have worked a set dollar amount based on their contribution. A citizen can apply for social security (retirement) at the age of 62, to receive 80% of retirement benefits, or at the age of 65 to receive 100% of their benefit amount. At the age of 65 the government offers Medicaid to assist elderly persons with medical insurance, *more information about Medicaid is covered in Chapter 6.*

Persons experiencing difficulty collecting social security may find the following resource helpful for locating assistance: **The National Organization of Social Security Claimants' Representatives** 6 Prospect Street - Midland Park, NJ 07432-1691 (800) 431-2804 www.nosscr.org

For those who desire an early retirement before the age of 65, verify the conditions for early retirement with your retirement savings administrator (for persons with retirement savings plans like 401(k), Roth IRA's, and SEP's). It's easier to do more when there is sufficient money to cover costs for living; however, this is not true of all retirees. Many people opt to stop working for money to form non-profit organizations that assist others. Some choose not work to assist their families who need their experience and love. The following are resources to persons who are considering retiring:

Location	Source	
Books	Salisbury, Dallas and Marc Robinson. *Managing Money in Retirement.* Dorling Kindersley Publishing Inc., © 2000. Stephen, Rosenberg, CFP. *Last Minute Retirement Planning.* Career Press, Inc., © 1999.	
Web	www.agenet.com www.friendly4seniors.com www.eldernet.com www.spry.org	
Agencies	Medic Alert Foundation 2323 Colorado Ave. Turlock, CA 95382 (800) 432-5378 Spry Foundation 10 G Street. NE, Suite 600 Washington, DC 20002 (202) 216-0401	Lifeline Systems Incorporated 111 Lawrence St. Farmingham, MA 01702-8156 (800) 543-3546

I'M READY TO RETIRE, NOW WHAT DO I DO?

Your age, taxable savings, tax-exempt savings, and/or retirement accounts dictate what age you retire and what to do. A few people made large sums of money during the dot-com boom are able to retire at the age of 19. However, most people work hard for many years at companies and retire at the times when they're eligible to receive their retirement funds. 401(k) plans allow participants make tax-exempt withdrawals between the ages of 59½-70½ or the age of 55 if you took an early retirement (ask your plan administrator for information regarding your 401(k) plan). People who have reached, or are nearing the age of 62 can begin withdrawing 80% of their funds from social security. Those who are 65 and older are eligible to receive full retirement benefits. All persons approaching their 65th birthday should apply for Medicare, regardless of the age you plan to retire; your medical benefits become available at age 65 and do not increase so it is beneficial to begin collecting medical benefits. People who have waited to retire at the age of 70 receive an increased social security retirement amount (as they have paid more into their fund). Unlike social security, those with retirement plans such as 401(k) must begin withdrawing from their retirement accounts, or attract a 50% excise tax from the IRS for not withdrawing the minimal set amounts.

Location	Source	
Books	Egans, Hom and Barbara Wagner. *I'M Retiring, Now What?*! Zoul Silver Lining Books, © 2001. Orman, Suze & Linda Mead. *You've Earned It, Don't Lose It*. Newmarket Press, © 1997. Stan, Hinde. *How to Retire Happy.* McGraw Hill Text, © 2001.	
Web	www.retireonyourterms.com www.retireonyourterms.com www.retire.net www.aarp.org	
Agencies	**American Saving Council** 2121 K Street, NW Suite 600 Washington, DC (202) 659-0670	**Social Security Administration Office of Public Inquires** 6401 Security Blvd. Room 4-C-5 Annex

Location	Source
	Baltimore, MD
Social Security	21235
Administration	(800) 772-1213
Baltimore, MD 21235	
(410) 956-2736	
(800) 772-1213	

LEGAL RESOURCES FOR SENIORS

Seniors are often found the target of scams from callous business people pushing fraudulent goods. Some brutes physically attack seniors, as they are often weaker and have frail health. Seniors must protect themselves by researching their investment options and wisely evaluating those who occupy their lives, as family members and close friends have been know to commit many crimes against elderly relatives. However, take comfort in knowing that the courts are hard on criminals who target seniors. Outstanding attorneys fight for the rights of senior citizens and defend them when crimes occur. Your local senior citizenship center is an excellent source for locating legal resources. Members often share their good and bad experiences with others. Referral organizations offer free information regarding legal resources as well as free or low-cost legal clinics.

Location	Source
Book	Love, Tiffany R. *Leveling The Playing Field: Senior Resources.* Petra © 2003.
Web	www.consumerlaw.org www.aapr.org

Location	Source
	www.abanet.org/elderly www.usdoj.gov www.eldernet.com www.elderweb.com www.nsclc.org
Agencies	**Federal Trade Commission** 600 Pennsylvania Avenue, NW Washington, DC 20580 (877) FTC-HELP (382-4357) (202) 326-2222 (617) 523-8010 **Eldercare Initiative in Consumer Law** National Consumer Law Center Inc. 18 Tremont Street, Suite 400 Boston, MA 02108 **National Senior Citizens Law Center** 1101 14th Street, Suite 400 Washington, DC 20005 (202) 289-6976	**Legal Counsel for the Elderly (LCE)** American Association of Retired Persons 601 E Street, NW Washington, DC 20049 (202) 434-2120 **American Bar Association** Commission on the Legal Problems of the Elderly 740 15th Street, NW Washington, DC 20005-1022 (202) 662-8690 **Department of Justice** 950 Pennsylvania Avenue, NW Washington, DC 20530 (202) 514-2000

HOUSING

Persons who are 55 or older have many housing options available to them like retirement communities for independent seniors, senior apartments for those on a fixed income, assisted living facilities, nursing homes for those who require round the clock care. For those who own their own home and desire to sell to purchase another for greater value there is a tax credit program that is available, ask a knowledgeable broker for details. This section provides resource information to all of the hosing options listed above.

Location	Source	
Web	www.seniorsite.com www.senioresources.com www.mapleknoll.org www.livon.com www.newlifestyles.com www.elderweb.com	
Agencies	**Elder Web** 1305 Chadwick Drive Normal, IL 61761 (309) 451-3319 **Eldercare Locator** (800) 677-1116	**Federal Consumer Information Center** P.O. Box 100 Pueblo, CO 81009 (888) 878-3256 (888) 688-9889 (800) 326-2996 (TTY)

Locating Housing for Low-Income Seniors

Even with the assistance of retirement funds and social security one may quickly find out that they are barely meeting their financial needs. Most money is spent on housing. Housing in Urban Development (HUD) has programs available for seniors to offset housing costs. Programs like section 8 and section 201 (funding entirely for senior residences) prove to be valuable to those on fixed incomes requiring independent residences. In addition, public housing is available for senior residences as well as low-income persons, which may be convenient for seniors who care for younger family members as most of the senior residences are strictly for seniors and their spouses.

Public Housing

Public housing has attracted many low-income residents as well as seniors who both rely on affordable housing. The units are federally funded, but owned and operated by local public housing authorities. A person can reside in public housing as long as he/she meets the financial requirements based on their family size and abides by the housing authorities rules.

Location	Source	
Web	www.strokeassociation@heart.org www.catholiccharitiesusa.org www.aoanet.org www.povertylaw.org www.senioresources.com www.seniorsite.com www.aahsa.org www.hrsa.gov/osp/dfer www.thegeezer.com www.greenthumb.org	
Agencies	**Hill-Burton Free Medical Care Program** Health Resources and Services Administration Department of Health and Human Services Division of Facilities Compliance and Recovery 5600 Fisher Lane Room 10C-16 Rockville, MD 20857 (800) 638-0742	**Foundation of American ACAD/Ophthalmology** National Eye Care Project P.O. Box 429098 San Francisco, CA 94142-9098 **Green Thumb, Inc.** 2000 North 14th Street, Suite 800

Location	Source	
	(800) 492-0359 (MD Only)	Arlington, VA 22201
		(703) 522-7272
	Catholic Charities USA	
	1731 King Street, Suite 200	**American Stroke**
		Association
	Alexandria, VA 22314	c/o American Heart
	(703) 549-1390	Association
		7272 Greenville Ave
		Dallas, TX 75231
	National Center on	(888) 4Stroke
	Poverty Law, Inc.	(888) (478-7653)
	205 West Monroe	
	Chicago, IL 60606	**American Optometric**
	(312) 263-3830	**Association (AOA)**
	.	243 North Lindberg Blvd
		St Louis, MO 63141

Assisted Living Senior Homes

Throughout the country communities have been constructed to address the needs of seniors. Senior homes provide easy access for residences, with elevator use, medical personnel available throughout the day to assist members, and/or transportation to and from medical facilities as well as a host of other amenities. The costs for living in these homes vary depending on the property management company; however, units that receive government funding take section 8 vouchers. The number of senior home varies depending on the state and city.

Location	Source	
Web	www.mapleknoll.org	www.alfa.org
	www.retirementdirectory.com	www.jcaho.org

Location	Source	
	www.aaha.org www.Assistedlivingonline.com www.ahca.org	www.nachc.com www.alfa.org
Agencies	**American Association of Homes and Services for the Aging** 2519 Connecticut Avenue, NW Washington, DC 20008-1520 (202) 783-2242 **American Health Care Association (AHCA)** 1201 L Street, NW Washington, DC 20005-4014 (800) 321-0343 **Administration on Aging** Wilbur J. Cohen Building 330 Independence Ave, SW Washington, DC 20201 (800) 677-1116	**Joint Commission on Accreditation of Health Care Organization** (800) 994-6610 **Assisted Living Federation of America** 11200 Waples Mill Road, Suite 150 Fairfax, VA 22030 (703) 691-8100 **National Association of Community Health Centers** 1330 New Hampshire Avenue, NW, Suite 122 Washington, DC 20036 (202) 659-8008

Nursing Homes

Aging often brings on physical burdens that require the assistance of trained personnel 24-hours a day. Alternatives like senior homes, which often offer part-time, nursing care, may not meet the needs of persons who are no longer able to care for themselves. Nursing homes have received a lot of attention over the past 10-15 years for subjecting residences to horrific conditions. Federal and state laws were enacted to ensure the protection and swift prosecution of nursing home management companies and their staff who do not operate safe, clean, and responsive environments. Even with such legislation it is imperative that persons select responsible homes for love ones.

Location	Sources	
Web	www.retirementdirectory.com www.aahsa.org www.Assistedlivingonline.com www.alfa.org www.nacha.com www.ahea.org www.careguide.com www.nursinghomealert.com	
Agencies	**Assisted Living Federation of America** 11200 Waples Mill Road, Suite 150 Fairfax, VA 22030 (703) 691-8100 **American Association Of Home And Services for the Aging** 2519 Connecticut Avenue, NW Washington, DC 20008-1520 (202) 783-2242	**American Health Care Association (AHCA)** 1201 L Street, NW Washington, DC 20005-4014 (800) 321-0343

HOME HEALTH CARE

Seniors who own a home yet require medical assistance may find home health care to be a valuable alternative to living in

308

a nursing home. Home health care provides nursing assistance to persons in need of medical attention at their home. Not only is nursing assistance provided, but physical therapy, day care services (for those seniors who should not be left home alone), and cooking services to name a few. Home health workers bath the patient, clean living areas, and tend to the patients overall health needs.

Location	Sources	
Web	www.careguide.com www.vnaa.org www.nahc.org www.americangeriatrics.org	
Agencies	**American Geriatrics Society (AGS)** 350 Fifth Avenue New York, NY 10118 (212) 308-1414 **American Association for Geriatrics Psychiatry (AAGP)** 7910 Wood Mont Avenue, Suite 1050 Bethesda, MD 20814-3004 (301) 654-7850 **American Counseling Association (ACA)** 5999 Stevenson Ave. Alexandria, VA 22304 (800) 347-6647	**National Association for Home Health Care** 228 7th Street, SE Washington, DC 20003 (202) 547-7424 **Visiting Nurse Association of America** 11 Beacon Street Boston, MA 02108 (888) 866-8773

ESTATE PLANNING

Persons who did not adopt the *die broke* philosophy and actually have an estate to leave must find it a priority to plan how their estate is managed in the event of incapacitation or death. Be aware of and legal pitfalls to avoid in order to effectively execute ones desire. Certified estate planners can assist persons with organizing their estate, although the majority of people do not require such attention. This section provides resources and explanation of basic terms for estate planning. In addition, there are resources listed below that assist those needing more information.

Location	Source
Books	Clifford, Dennis and Cora Jordan [Attorney's]. *Plan Your Estate.* Nolo. © 2000. Sandy F. Kraemer. *60 Minute Estate Planning.* Prentice Hall Press, © 1999. Edmund, Fleming T. *Estate Planning & Administration.* Allworth Press. © 2001.
Web	www.estateattorney.com www.estateweb.com www.estateplanning.com www.estateplanningcenter.com www.financiallearning.com

Advance Directive

An advance directive is a document that instructs practitioners and family on what decisions to make in the event you become incapacitated. Documenting your wishes in case of resuscitation, life support, brain death, heart attack, etc. are topics covered in the advance directive. In addition, a limited power of attorney should be considered to handle certain/limited affairs in the event of debilitation. The document can be an informal handwritten sheet of paper or a ten page notarized legal document. As long as the patient signs, it is a legal document (notarizing is recommended). Nonetheless, the patient has the right to change their mind at any point.

The Advance Directive should be on file with the hospital or medical practitioners office, to avoid delay in carrying out your desires. All persons should have an advance directive, especially those with estates in order to circumvent the court appointing a conservator for your property. It can be as simple or complicated as you like; it's your desire but it cannot contain anything illegal.

Wills

Wills document the dispersing of personal property after death. Anyone can create a will without hiring an attorney unless your estate is worth a significant amount and there are many complicated matters. Wills should be typed or printed from a computer by persons over the age of 18 who are of sound mind. The will should bear a witness signature and/or be notarized. Excellent self-help books and online resources are available for documenting wishes for your estate after death.

Location	Source
	Condon, Gerald M. *Beyond the Grave: The Right Way and the Wrong Way of Leaving Money to Your Children*. Harper Business ©1996.

Location	Source
	Croke, Frank J., William F. Croke, *Family Trusts : Financial Errors in Trusts, How to Avoid and Correct Them, Provide for Your Family, Save Taxes, Protect Your Assets and Avoid Probate* (2nd Edition). Capital Management Press © 2000. Alexander A. BoveHenry *The Complete Book of Wills, Estates & Trusts (2nd Edition).* Holt © 2000. Robert L. Mennell *Wills and Trusts in a Nutshell* West Wadsworth © 1994.
Web	www.itslegal.com www.nolo.com www.quicken.com

Living Trusts

Living trusts also called *intervivous* allows a person, the trustee, to control property (land, money, jewelry, etc) for beneficiaries until the time of death. At the time of death property is distributed according to the terms of the trust. Once all property is distributed to heirs the trust is ended. A person can be the trustee to his or her own estate, and explicitly appoint another trustee at the time of death. Living trusts are excellent methods to avoiding probate, as property transferred into the living trust does not go through probate; they can be

Most banks have pay to upon death forms for members use in order to avoid delays in paying beneficiaries. Similarly, auto lenders honor transfer upon death demand statements from borrowers.

created relatively inexpensively by a paralegal, unless the estate is enormous and/or complicated.

Location	Source	
	Condon, Gerald M. esq. and Jeffery L. Condon, esq. *Beyond The Grave: The right Way and The Wrong Way of Leaving Money to Your Children (and others).* Revised Edition Harper Business, © 2001. Shenkman, Martin M. *The Complete Living Trusts Program.* John Wiley & Sons, Inc., © 2000.	Abts, Henry W. III *The Living Trust.* Contemporary Publishing Group, Inc., ©1989. Espert, Robert A., Renno L. Peterson, and David K. Cahoone, *The Living Trust Workbook.* Penguin Putnam Inc., © 2001.
Books		
Web	www.completetrust.com www.nolo.com www.metlife.com	

LIFE INSURANCE

Purchasing life insurance is quite costly and the cost increases depending on age. Organizations exist to assist seniors, or anyone interested, with selecting the best policy for their needs. The following help is offered:

Location	Source
Web	www.insweb.com www.insurance.com www.lowestinsurancerates.com www.insurancefraud.org www.insurancefraud.org www.insure.com

Location	Source
	www.reliaquote.com www.e-analytics.com
Agencies	**American Council of Life Insurers** 1001 Pennsylvania Ave, NW Suite 500 South Washington, DC 20004-2599 (800) 942-4242

ALZHEIMER'S

Alzheimer is a disease that affects the brain. The exact cause is unknown and many speculations exist. Family members are the best resources for person with Alzheimer's, as they are able to care for aging loved ones for a small fraction of the costs of nursing and assisted living homes. Families place loved ones in facilities that specialize in treating Alzheimer patients because of the emotions of watching your loved one deteriorate. The following resources are available to persons affected with Alzheimer's and their loved ones.

Location	Sources	
Books	Warner, Mark L. *The Complete Guide to Alzheimer's-Proofing Your Home.* Purdue University Press © 2000. Mace, Nancy L., Peter V. Rabins. *The 36-Hour Day : A Family*	Strauss, Claudia J. *Talking to Alzheimer's: Simple Ways to Connect When You Visit with a Family Member or Friend.* © New Harbinger Pubns © 2002.

Location	Sources	
	Guide to Caring for Persons With Alzheimer Disease, Related Dementing Illnesses, and Memory Loss in Later Life. Warner Books © 2001.	
Web	www.alzwell.com www.alz.org www.alzheimers.org	www.mapleknoll.org www.ahaf.org
Agencies	**Alzheimer Association** 919 N. Michigan Ave. Suite 1100 Chicago, IL 60611-1676 (800) 272-3900 (312) 335-8882 (TTY) **Alzheimer's Disease Education And Referrals (ADEAR)** P. O. Box 8250 Silver Spring, MD 20907-8250 (800) 438-4380	**American Health Assistance Foundation (AHAF)** 15825 Shady Grove Road, Suite 140 Rockville, MD 20850 (800) 437-AHAF (437-2423)

AGING

The following resources provide information on aging in the American society. The web sites have links, which can direct interested persons to resources for *older* Americans.

Location	Source	
Web	www.agelessdesign.com www.asaging.org	www.aoa.dhhs.gov www.arclab.org
Agencies	**American Society on Aging (ASA)** 833 Market Street, Suite 511 San Francisco, CA 94103-1824 (415) 974-9600 **Foundation of American ACAD/Ophthalmology** National Eye Care Project P.O. Box 429098 San Francisco, CA 94142-9098 **Alliance for Aging Research** 2021 K Street, NW, Suite 305 Washington, DC 20006 (202) 293-2856	**National Institute on Aging** P.O. Box 8250 Silver Springs, MD 20907-8250 (800) 483-4380 **Administration on Aging** Department of Health and Human Services 330 Independence Avenue, SW Washington, DC 20201 (202) 619-7501 **Eldercare Locater:** (800) 677-1116

Chapter 15

Death and Dying

*I think those who were so ruthlessly murdered
on September 11 would want us to do better.
In their final moments they were calling
home, expressing love. The very least, and
most, we can do is the same. Right now.*
Oprah Winfrey

R ntly I assisted a friend dying of colon cancer. As this was
ntionally difficult, it was a learning experience that is
nedded in the fabric of my soul. Death and Dying aren't
. With understanding, support and some preparation
this process can be very spiritual and meaningful to the
patient as well as love ones.

☼How The Information Was Found

The results provided were found based on answers given by Hospice workers and performing web research.

Persons who are dying have several quality books to choose from, however, not many web resources were located. Care options and family resources have more choices available.

Bereavement and specific forms of death are well covered on the Internet by web sites and online bookstores. Walk-in bookstores vary on the type of information provided, several books, <u>omitted</u> from this directory, were clinical and not useful. The books listed were chosen by referrals or by personal reading.

CARE CHOICES

Once you or a love one is diagnosed as terminally ill, care choices are immediately presented by the physician and/or a caseworker. As a standard of practice most hospitals have a caseworker (a trained social worker who looks after the emotional and physical needs of patients) onsite to assist with resources for the patient and family.

The caseworker arranges a meeting with the patient, doctor(s) and love ones to discuss treatment options and future care. The participants are considered the patients care team members. Loved ones should regard their attendance as a high honor, as you are the ones who have been selected to provide the needed support during their last days.

Prior to the meeting it is important to locate as much information as possible on their condition and prognosis. Refrain from emotional outbursts and focus mainly on the information presented by the physician and caseworker. Keep in mind that the patient is more than likely aware of their prognosis and for the remainder of their life they will be coming to terms with releasing their present form. If the physician presents alternative treatments write it down and investigate it later. Ask as many questions as you like. You should leave the meeting having all of your questions answered and feeling certain on the next course of action. Some options presented by practitioners are; continue current treatment, alternative treatments, home health care, and hospice care.

The patient may decide to continue with the current treatment plan. This may include aggressive chemotherapy, radiation, surgery, dialysis, and a host of medical treatment options. These options are initially presented to the patient. He/she is given time to think over the information. Prior to the meeting, if circumstances are optimal, the physician should present the most effective treatment option to the least effective. Blood tests, X-rays, MRI's, CT scans, biopsies, etc. should have been performed prior to the physician's recommendation(s). Knowing this data is vital to determining the course of future treatment.

The physician should confidently know the patient's medical history, and prognosis prior to discussing their future. Patients can request a copy of their medical chart, all patients are entitled to a copy upon request. Should you seek another opinion, having knowledge of their medical history is extremely helpful to another physician.

Traditional Medicine

The pros to continuing with modern medical treatment are the results of studies conducted prior to their approval by the FDA (food and drug administration) The data is reliable and provides ease of mind. Also, they may prove to have favorable results with prolonging life. However, it is uncertain as to the quality of life one will have after the treatment has completed.

The cons are the side affects and the quality of life. Discuss these issues with the physician for each option presented. Most physicians are not able to predict what will occur after the treatment. However, physicians who specialize in the field and have experience can to provide information on patients who were in a similar circumstance and speak of their outcome.

Alternative Treatment

Alternative treatments have had great successes. However, this is difficult to prove, as *modern* medical science does not endorse alternative treatment programs. This should not overrule the effectiveness of alternative treatment plans, which can be a combination of both approved medical treatments and those that are being studied. For an example, there are many chemotherapy treatment options that are currently being studied. A physician can recommend that a non-participating patient receive the experimental drug if the study is receiving favorable results from the participants, this is a form of alternative treatment. Patients can investigate the treatment options on their own and inform their doctor of the findings. Physicians should seriously consider this as an option and if found true, take strides to fervently work on their patient's behalf, which may include going directly to FDA for acceptance into the program.

Hospice care

Hospice care is palliative care for patients who have been diagnosed with a terminal illness, which means that their prognosis for life is less than six months. Once a patient has enrolled into a hospice program, a caseworker from the program meets with the patient and physician even if the patient is hospitalized. During the initial visit a registered nurse assess the patient to ascertain his/her condition, mental state (including the acceptance of their condition), and physical needs. The hospice team orders the appropriate equipment for the patient if he/she will be transported to a home. If the patient is not able to return home (or to the home of a love one) then the hospice worker coordinates an alternative location for the patient. This is an uncomfortable time for the patient as he or she is more than likely ready to leave the hospital, but is uncertain about the duration of their life. Having the support of loved is vital during this period.

Hospice is not only beneficial to the patient but to their love ones as well; they offer grief counseling, family meetings to discuss the patient' status, Chaplin services, nursing, and a host of resources. Hospice does not provide aggressive treatment; they are present to comfort the patient during the process of dying. This includes, but is not limited to offering pain medications, oxygen, continued IV treatments, emotional support, training to care givers and a host of services that offer comfort to the patient. The extent of the services may be defined on a case-by-case basis. Hospice care workers are trained in CPR, but do not perform artificial resuscitation in the event a patients stops breathing; they are present to help the patient be as comfortable as possible during the dying process.

What if the patient lives beyond six months?

It's important to note that some patients live much longer than six months and some recover. Hospice will continue until the patient's physician determines that it is no longer necessary or the patient electively chooses to leave the program.

Location	Resources
Book	Doyle, Derek, David Jeffrey, Kenneth Calman. *Palliative Care in the Home*. Oxford University Press © 2000.

Location	Resources	
Web	www.hospicefoundation.org www.hospice.org www.nho.org www.rights.org www.hospicepatients.org www.chionline.org www.americanhospice.org	
Agencies	**Children's Hospice International** 901 North Pitt Street Suite 230 Alexandria, VA 22314 (800) 2-4-CHILD **Hospice Patients Alliance** 4541 Gemini Street P.O. BOX 744 Rockford, MI 49341-0744 **National Hospice and Palliative Care Organization** 700 Diagonal Road Suite 625 Alexandria, VA 22314 (703) 837-1500 **Children's Hospice International** 2202 Mt. Vernon Ave. Suite 3C Alexandria, VA 22301 (800) 242-4453	**American Hospice Foundation** 2120 L Street, NW Suite 200 Washington, DC 20037 (202) 223-0204 **National Institute for Jewish Hospice** 8631 W. 3rd St. Suite 210E Los Angeles, CA 90048 (310) 854-3036 **Starlight Children's Foundation** 1900 Avenue of the Stars Suite 739 Century City, CA 90067 (800) 950-9474 **Children's Wish Foundation** (800) 323-9474 Hospice Link 190 Westbrook Rd. Essex, CT 06426-1510 (800) 767-1620

Some managed care plans cover the costs for hospice care. Contact a medical representative or broker for more information regarding specific treatment and care covered. Medical and Medicare cover the cost of hospice care. Given the patients terminal illness, the application for medical is often expedited to ensure approval prior to their release from the hospital.

HOME HEALTH CARE FOR TERMINAL PATIENTS

Home health is desirable for people who are ill, disabled, or elderly and wish to live in their own homes, or with love ones as opposed to a health care facility; it's ideal for those desiring aggressive care. Home health workers administer oral medications under physician orders; they provide personal care services and general housekeeping; they operate similarly to hospice expect hospice is palliative care (non evasive) care specialized for terminal illness. Home health care workers are trained in CPR and can administer in the event a patient stops breathing.

Considering Home Health Care

Home health care is ideal for patients who are seeking and/or undergoing aggressive treatment but wish to do so in the comfort of home.

Location	Source
Book	E. Quill, Timothy. *Caring for Patients at the End of Life: Facing an Uncertain Future Together.* Oxford University Press © 2001.
Web	www.ltc-resources.com www.nahc.org www.hcaa-homecare.com www.aahomecare.org www.longtermcare-hotline.com
Agencies	**American Association For Home Care** 625 Slaters Lane Suite 200 Alexandria, VA 22314 (703) 836-6263 **National Association for Home Care** 228 Seventh Street, SE, Washington, DC 20003 (202) 547-7424 **Home Care Association of America** 9570 Regency Square Blvd Jacksonville, FL 32225 (904-)725-7100

Funeral Arrangements

It's a beneficial for persons to express their wishes in writing as to what should be done with their remains, where donations (flowers, monies, gifts, etc.) should be sent, and precise funeral arrangements. This information must not be placed in a will, which is often located and read weeks after the funeral. Persons with advance directives can include a statement in the document like: *In the event of my death I wish to be immediately cremated and I do not want an autopsy performed.* This simple statement can end worry from family members who spend hours and days attempting

325

to make the *right* choices. Since an advance directive is (at least it should be) on file with the hospital, family members have immediate access to understanding your wishes during a crisis. Having an accessible folder with the final arrangement plans is also an excellent idea.

Location	Source
Book	James, Malcolm and Victoria Lynn *A Funeral Planning Manual and Survivors Guide.* Mavami Inc. © 2000.
Web	www.nfda.org www.lovingeulogies.com www.casketstores.com/Links.htm www.funerals.org www.cremation.org
Agencies	**National Funeral Directors Association** 13625 Bishops Drive Brookfield, WI 53005 (800) 228-6332 **Funeral Consumers** P.O. Box 10 Hinesburg, Vermont 05461 802-482-3437 **Shugar's Publishing** **The Purple Directory (African-American Funeral Homes)** P.O. Box 38665 Detroit, MI 48238-0665 (313) 836-8600 (800) 377-9129

I'M DYING

Typically a physician diagnoses your condition as terminally ill (meaning you have less than six months to live). This is not the final verdict, getting a second, third, or fourth opinion often reveals health care options that are not performed by the attending physician. Many stories are told of persons with terminal conditions who have undergone special treatment and have survived. Special conditions exist for each story · consult your physician or the facility conducting the study for more information. Recently I read a story of a woman with a stage four, terminal, cancer who received FDA approval to take an experimental drug. The medication worked and she is alive today. I have also read about and seen people exhausting all of their resources to stay alive, even forfeiting the opportunity to live the remainder of their lives enjoying family and friends in exchange for panaceas that leave loved ones emotionally torn at the time of their death.

Communicating with love ones about your condition whether a cure is pursued or not helps loved ones heal from the passing of the person they dearly love. At some point each of use must vacate our temporary shells. Watching ones body deteriorate requires a constant stream of strength from supportive love ones to see you through. Communication is key during this process. Tell them when you're in pain, uncomfortable, angry, or sad. Those who care for you need to know how you feel both physically and emotionally-they want you to be comfortable. At a stage in this process you may be unable to communicate effectively, or not at all. Your caretakers must be able to decipher your expressions and know what they mean in order to help.

As the dying process continues you will begin reflecting on your life in greater detail. Remembrance of events that have been so long forgotten, but have shaped your behavior become anew. People who you haven't seen in years will appear to offer soft words of love, some of these people you may not want to see, but most will be a comfort to your soul. You do not have to accept visits from everyone who wants to say goodbye. Feel comfortable in knowing that some people wont understand, but this process is entirely about your life and not about selfish desires a person may have.

Location	Source	
Books	Byock M.D., Ira. *Dying Well: Peace and Possibilities at the End of Life.* Riverhead Books ©1998. Singh, Kathleen Dowling. *The Grace in Dying : How We Are Transformed Spiritually as We Die.* Harper San Francisco © 2000.	Lynn, Joanne. *Handbook for Mortals: Guidance for People Facing Serious Illness.* EditorOxford University Press ©1999. Furman, Joan. *The Dying Time: Practical Wisdom for the Dying and Their Caregivers.* © 1997.
Web	www.thirteen.org/bid	

PROBATE

Probate is the process of distributing a person, who has died, assets and paying creditors. Many states mandate probate court when a person has an estate worth a considerable amount. A court appointed administrator ensures that the terms in the will are carried out if a will exist. This process is very expensive and takes several months to resolve before heirs receive their inheritance. It's wise to avoid probate by drafting a living trust and naming beneficiaries on polices and accounts. Wills provide detail as to who will receive what property, living trusts distributes the property prior to death thereby avoiding probate. For information on locating attorneys consider the web resources below in addition to those mentioned in Chapter 11.

Location	Source	
Book	Appel, Jens C. III, F. Burce Gentry. *The Complete Probate Kit.* John Wiley & Sons © 1991. Appel, Jens C., F. Bruce Gentry, *The Complete Probate Kit.* John Wiley & Sons © 1991.	Jurinski, James John. *Probate and Settling an Estate: Step-By-Step.* Barrons Educational Series © 1997.
Web	www.abanet.org/rppt/publications/magazine/home.html www.nolo.com www.estateplanningattorneyatwills.com	

Organ Donations

Persons donating their organs have saved lives around the world. Typically donors are those who were otherwise healthy but encountered a tragic accident that left them incapacitated. With permission from the individual (donor card or advance directive) or family, doctors remove certain vital organs. Those in need of organs or desire to donate remains can inquire from the following resources

Location	Source	
Web	www.adec.org www.compassionbooks.com www.rights.org	
Agencies	**Association for Death Education and Counseling** 342 North Main Street West Hartford, CT 06117-2507 (860) 586-7503 **The Living Bank** (800) 528-2971	**United network Of Organ Sharing** (888) TXINFO1 **National Marrow Donor Program** (800) 627-7692

SUPPORT FOR LOVE ONES OF DYING PATIENTS

To spare oneself from grief at all cost can be achieved only at the price of total detachment, which excludes the ability to experience happiness.
Erich Fromm

Being present when a love one dies is an honor. It's comforting to see them make resolve with their life. When they are unable to speak an unexplainable peace over takes their being as the last hours near. As this metamorphosis occurs a since of calm inhabits the room where they lie. One cannot help but to feel honor for being present.

When a love one is dying and can communicate, take this time to share what he/she means to you. Encourage other family and friends to do the same. Allow your love one to express their thoughts about you, this will be console after their passing. Cherish holding their warm hand filled with life · enjoy the moments. If there are deep-seated issues, then attempt to resolve them and find understanding to help with insight into their state. This is a critical juncture in the life of every person affected by this process; each person is uniquely touched, as each relationship is different.

Location	Source
Books	Callanan, Maggie. *Patricia Kelley Final Gifts: Understanding the Special Awareness, Needs, and Communications of the Dying.* Bantam Books © 1997. Furman, Joan. *The Dying Time: Practical Wisdom for the Dying and Their Caregivers.* Random House © 1997.
Web	www.ntcacares.org www.wellspouse.org www.mowaa.org www.elderhope.com www.growthhouse.org
Agencies	**Meals On Wheels Association Of America** 1414 Prince Street Suite 302 Alexandria, VA 22314 (703) 548-5558 **AIDS MEMORIAL QUILT** The NAMES Project 2362 Market Street	**Well Spouse Foundation** 30 East 40th Street New York, NY 10016 (800) 838-0879 **National Family Caregivers Association** 1400 Connecticut

Location	Source
San Francisco, CA 94114-9926 (415) 863-5511	Ave. #500 Kensington, MO 20895-3944 (800) 896-3650

SUICIDE AND DEPRESSION

As difficult as it to overcome the grief of a loved one that dies because of accident or disease, those who die due to suicide is distressing to friends and family; it's difficult to understand why the person opted to take their life – the ubiquitous question of *what could have been done to prevent their death* remains unanswered. Family members who watch their distress often feel helpless or tortured by the thought that one day they will kill themselves. The resources below are for family and friends of persons who have committed suicide.

People considering suicide oftentimes abandon the hope for overcoming current and future problems that time holds. Problems do occur and they don't go away. But time does leave and with its passing an opportunity to turn the next challenge into a hurdle to be overcome - not with physical strength but with perseverance, until problems cease to preoccupy your life, more so enjoyment. If the object of your enjoyment is no longer present, then draw upon your creativity to spur forward.

Location	Source	
Web	http://depression.cmhc.com www.depressionfallout.com www.depressionalliance.org www.covenanthouse.org www.hopeforhealing.org www.yellowribbon.org	www.teenanswer.org www.befrienders.org www.afsp.org www.save.org www.depression.org
Agencies	**American Society for Suicide Prevention National** 120 Wall Street, 22ND Floor New York, NY 10005 (888) 333-AFSP **Alliance for Mentally Ill** 2107 Wilson Blvd. Suite 3rd Floor Arlington, VA 22201 (800) 950-6264 **Depression Awareness** (800) 421-4211 **National Foundation for Depressive Illness** P. O. Box 2257 New York, NY 10116 (800) 248-4344 **New Hope Online Counseling** Crystal Cathedral 12141 Lewis St. Garden Grove, CA 92840 (714) 639-4673 (714) New-Hope	**National Youth Crisis Hotline** (800) 448-4663 **Girls And Boys Town National Hotline** (800) 448-3000 (800) 448-1833 (TDD) **Answer (Adolescents Never Suicide When Everyone Responds)** Mental Health Association of the Heartland 739 Minnesota Avenue Kansas City, KS 66101 (800) 784-2433 **National Family Support of Mental Ill** (800) 628-1696

333

Location	Source	
	SOLOS, Inc. (Survivor of Loved Ones' Suicides) PO Box 592 Dumfries, VA 22026-0592	**National Referral Center** 222 W. Ball Rd. Anaheim, CA 92805 (800) 530-0467

BEREAVEMENT

... bereavement is a universal and integral part of our experience of love.
        C. S. Lewis

Missing and grieving loved ones is part of our experience. A universal method to bereavement doesn't exist; some do not blink at the passing of friend or family member, while others take as much time as they need to mourn. Loosing someone who is special and dear, who contributed to the development of our lives can be astonishing. Whether taking time off or returning to *normal* actives, mourning does not change.

Location	Source
Books	Rando, Therese A. Ph.D. *How to Go on Living When Someone You Love Dies.* Bantam Books © 1991. Feinber, Linda Sones *I'm Grieving As Fast As I Can: How Young Widows and Widowers Can Cope and Heal.* New Horizon Press © 1994. Walton, Charlie, *When There Are No Words: Finding Your Way to Cope With Loss and Grief.* Pathfinder Publishing © 1996

Location	Source
Web	www.depressionfallout.com
	www.AFSP.org
	www.giveyourvoice.com
	www.griefnet.org
	www.growthhouse.org
	www.death-dying.com
	www.adultsiblinggrief.com
	www.counselingstlouis.net
	www.nfda.org/resources/grief.html
	www.thebereavementjourney.com
	www.widowsource.com

My love one has died

No words can to console a grieving heart, with time and support ones grief lessons. Time spent during bonding, loving, caring for, and understanding your love one will become bandage to a torn heart. Knowing that valuable time was spent learning about one another whether or not their were disagreements is essential to welcoming the change of their physical absence. Do not to dwell on disagreements and arguments, as this will not be any console. Focus on the memories that revealed insight into your love one. Find out how much they revealed about themselves and how much they learned about you. Their final words are remembered forever.

CANCERS

Persons diagnosed with cancer tend to want information pertinent to their diagnosed cancer. The web sites listed below have detailed information about specific types of cancers, valuable to those who have been diagnosed. For information regarding cancer I logged onto the American Cancer Society™ web page, which has comprehensive information including explanation of prognosis, nutrition,

335

links to other sites, as well as detail information about everything one needs to know about a specific cancer.

Location	Source	
Web	www.cancerpage.com www.cancerdirectory.com www.breastcancer.net www.skincancer.org	www.cancer.org www.cancer411.com www.cancerkids.org
Agencies	**ACS (American Cancer Society) National Cancer Information Center** (800) 227-2345 **Cancer Hope Network** (877) HOPE-NET **The Skin Cancer Foundation** 245 Fifth Avenue New York, NY 10016 (800) Skin490 (754-6490) **Candle Lighters Childhood Cancer Foundation** (800) 366-2223 **National Coalition for Cancer Research** 2300 North Street, NW Washington, DC 20004 **USTOO International** (800) 808-7866	**Cancer Information Service** **National Cancer Institute** (800) 422-6237 (800) 4-CANCER **Cancer Conquers Foundation** P.O. Box 238 Hershey, PA 17033 (800) 238-6499 **Y-ME National Breast Cancer Organization** 212 W. Buren St. 5th Floor Chicago, IL 60607 **National Bone Marrow Transplant Link** (800) 546-5268

AIDS/HIV

Persons are often affected by the negative stigma of AIDS, however being around others who understand your love for the individual and not the condition is helpful to living the last days in peace. Organizations and support groups exist for the patient as well as family members who need support and non-judgment during their last days.

Location	Source	
Books	Schoub, Barry D. *AIDS & HIV in Perspective: A Guide to Understanding the Virus and Its Consequences* 2nd Edition. Cambridge University Press, © 1999.	Ward, Darrell E., Mathilde, Krim. *The Amfar AIDS Handbook: The Complete Guide to Understanding HIV and AIDS*. W.W. Norton & Company, © 1998.
	Gifford, Allen, Kate Lorlg, Diane Laurent, Virginia M. Gonzalez, *Living Well With HIV and AIDS*. Bull Publishing Company, © 2000.	Broaden, Patricia, Haydeia Broadbent, Patricia Romanowski. *You Get Past the Tears: A Memoir of Love and Survival*. Villard Books, © 2002.
	Project Inform, et. Al. *The HIV Drug Book*. Pocket Books, © 1998.	Hawkins, Anne Hunsaker. *A Small, Good Thing: Stories of Children with HIV and Those Who Care for Them*. W.W. Norton & Company, © 2000.

Location	Source
Web	www.hellingwell.com/aids www.peoplewithaids.org/links.html#aids www.aoc.org www.infoweb.org www.hivatis.org www.stopaids.org www.magicjohnson.org www.aidsquilt.org www.songshine.com/hivinfo.html www.redcross.org/services/hss/hivaids http://nnlm.gov/pnr/samplers/afram_aids.html www.aidkids.org www.dishes.org www.projinf.org www.avert.org www.smartlink.net/~martinjh www.shanti.org www.blackaids.org
Agencies	**CDC National AIDS Clearinghouse** P.O. Box 6003 Rockville, MD 20849-6003 (800) 458-5231 (800) 243-7012 TTY/TDD **American Social Health Foundation** P.O. Box 13827 Research Triangle Park, NC 27709 AIDS English Hotline (800) 342-2437 Spanish AIDS Hotline (800) 342-7432 (800) 243-7889 TTY CDC STD Hotline (800) 227-8922	**CDC National Aids Hotline** (800) 342-2437 (English) (800) 344-7432 (Spanish) (800) 243-7889 (TTY) **AIDS Clinical Trials & Treatment** P. O. Box 6421 Rockville, MD 20849-6421 (800) 874-2572/ (800) TRAILS-A (800) 480-0440 TTY/TDD **American Red Cross/ HIV Education** (Consult with Local Agencies) National Headquarters 8111 Gatehouse Road JP6 Falls Church, VA 22042

Location	Source
	CAST Hotline (Center/Substance Abuse Treatment) Drug Abuse and AIDS (800) 622-4357	**Camp Laurel (for children living with HIV/AIDS)** P.O. Box 93204 Los Angeles, CA 90093 (323) 653-5005

MURDER/ VIOLENT DEATHS

Discovering that a loved one has died at the hands of someone who never beheld their inner beauty from watching them sit quietly or play peacefully arouses the utmost hatred a person can withstand. Immediately one desires to take revenge, to hurriedly end to life of the perpetrator(s): even their death does not relieve the anger and hurt felt by those who were touched by your loved ones life. Working through the grief is a daily exercise that requires support. Many counselors specialize in assisting those who loved ones die tragically and unexpectedly.

Location	Source
	Jenkins, Bill *What To Do When The Police Leave.* Insight Books © 2001.
Books	Noel, Brook, Pamela D. Blair, *I Wasn't Ready To Say Goodbye.* Champion Press © 2000.
Web	www.try-nova.org www.wakingtotears.com www.murdervictims.com www.survivorsofhomicide.com www.pomc.com

Location	Source	
Agencies	**MADD (Mothers Against Drunk Driving)** Parents of murdered Children 100 E. 8ᵗʰ Street Suite B-41 Cincinnati, OH 45202 (888-818-POMC) **National Organization for Victim Assistance (NOVA)** 717 D St. NW Washington, D.C. 20004 (202) 232-8560 / 24-hour Hot Line (202) 393-6683	**Tragedy Assistance Program for Survivors** 2001 S Street, NW Washington, DC 20009 (800) 959-TAPS **National Organization of Parents of Murdered Children** 100 East Eighth Street, Suite B-41 Cincinnati, Ohio 45202 (513) 721-5683

DEATH OF A PET

Pets are best friends and loving additions to human affection and love; they participate in our lives and provide a companionship that creates a bond that lasts for the duration of our lives; they are our love ones too. People refer to their pets as a son or daughter. When our baby's die, it is heart breaking and their life is deeply missed.

Location	Source
Books	Davis, Christine. *For Every Dog an Angel: The Forever Dog.* Lighthearted Press, © 1997.

Location	Source	
	Anderson, Moira K. *Coping With Sorrow on the Loss of Your Pet*. Alpine Publishers, © 1996. Kurz, Gary. *Cold Noses at the Pearly Gate*. Gary Kurz, © 1997	
Web	www.avma.org www.healthypet.com www.homevet.com www.in-memory-of-pets.com	www.petplace.com www.petplan.com www.aplb.org
Agencies	**American Veterinary Medical Association** 1931 North Meacham road Suite 100 Schaumburg, IL 60173-4360 **Association For Pet Loss Bereavement** P.O Box 106 Brooklyn, NY 11230 (718) 382-0690 **Miller Roth Animal Organization** 2000 E. Broadway - #141 Columbia, MO. 65201-6009 (573) 657-9633	**American Animal Hospital Association** 12575 W. Bayaud Ave. Lakewood, CO 80228 (303) 986-2800

341

Appendix A
EQUAL EMPLOYMENT OPPORTUNITY COMMISSION (EEOC)

If you believe you have been discriminated against by an employer, labor union or employment agency when applying for a job or while on the job because of your race, color, sex, religion, national origin, age, or disability, or believe that you have been discriminated against because of opposing a prohibited practice or participating in an equal employment opportunity matter, you may file a charge of discrimination with the U.S. Equal Employment Opportunity Commission (EEOC)

Title VII of the Civil Rights Act (Title VII) charges must be filed with EEOC within 180 days of the alleged discriminatory act. However, in states or localities where there is an anti-discrimination law and an agency authorized to grant or seek relief, a charge must be presented to that state or local agency.

Furthermore, in such jurisdictions, you may file charges with EEOC within 300 days of the discriminatory act, or 30 days after receiving notice that the state or local agency has terminated its processing of the charge, whichever is earlier. It is best to contact EEOC promptly when discrimination is suspected. When charges or complaints are filed beyond these time frames, you may not be able to obtain any remedy.

The EEOC enforces the following laws:
Title VII of the Civil Rights Act
Equal Pay Act of 1963
Age Discrimination Employment Act of 1967
Rehabilitation Act of 1973, Sections 501 and 505

Titles I and V of the Americans with Disabilities Act of 1990 (ADA)
Civil Rights Act of 1991

For more information regarding each of these Act's log onto the EEOC web site at: www.eeoc.gov/laws.html or contact a field office, *see the following section for address and telephone information.*

Contacting the EEOC

HEADQUARTERS

U.S. Equal Employment Opportunity Commission
1801 L Street, N.W.
Washington, D.C. 20507

Phone: (202) 663-4900
TTY: (202) 663-4494

FIELD OFFICES

To be automatically connected with the nearest EEOC field office, call:

Phone: 1-800-669-4000
TTY: 1-800-669-6820

Index

The Leveling The Playing Field Collection of Resources Guides

Order online at
www.Levelingtheplayingfield.com or toll-
free at (800) 986-6066

Order Form

Qty.	Title	Unit Price	Total
	Subtotal		
	CA residents add sales tax		
	Basic Shipping Discount (*$2.00* for 1 item; *$6.00* for 2 or more)		
	Rush Delivery (*$10.50*-any size order)*		
	Total		

Name

Address

(UPS to street address; Priority shipping to P.O. Boxes)
*Delivered in 3 business days from verification of order.

For Faster Service Use Your Credit Card and Order Online at
www.levelingtheplayingfield.com or toll free at (800) 986-6066

Order 24 hours a day

Fax your order

Email

Payment Method

☐ Check enclosed

☐ VISA   ☐ Master card   ☐ Discover Card   ☐ American Express

Account #   Expiration Date

Authorizing Signature

Daytime Phone

PRICES SUBJECT TO CHANGE.

Visit Us Online At: www.LevelingThePlayingField.com for currently releases